D0370451

Lake Mead National Recreation Area

AMERICA'S NATIONAL PARKS

Lake Mead National Recreation Area

A History of America's First National Playground

Jonathan Foster

UNIVERSITY OF NEVADA PRESS   Reno & Las Vegas

America's National Parks
Series Editor: Char Miller

University of Nevada Press, Reno, Nevada 89557 USA
www.unpress.nevada.edu
Copyright © 2016 by University of Nevada Press
All rights reserved
Manufactured in the United States of America
Cover design by Erin Kirk New

LIBRARY OF CONGRESS CATALOGING-IN-PUBLICATION DATA
Names: Foster, Jonathan, 1972– author.
Title: Lake Mead National Recreation Area : A History of America's First
National Playground / by Jonathan Foster.
Description: Reno : University of Nevada Press, [2016] | Series: America's
National Parks | Includes bibliographical references and index.
Identifiers: LCCN 2016004239 (print) | LCCN 2016005053 (ebook) |
ISBN 978-1-943859-15-3 (pbk. : alk. paper) |
ISBN 978-0-87417-005-4 (e-book)
Subjects: LCSH: Lake Mead National Recreation Area (Ariz. and Nev.)–History.
Classification: LCC F788 .F65 2016 (print) | LCC F788 (ebook) |
DDC 979.3/12–dc23
LC record available at http://lccn.loc.gov/2016004239

FIRST PRINTING

For Marianne, Nora, and Sadie

Contents

Illustrations

Abbreviations

BDRA	Boulder Dam Recreation Area
BLM	Bureau of Land Management
BMI	Basic Magnesium Industries
CCC	Civilian Conservation Corps
CDC	Colorado Development Company
EPA	Environmental Protection Agency
FERC	Federal Energy Regulatory Commission
IID	Imperial Irrigation District
LDS	The Church of Jesus Christ of Latter-day Saints
LMNRA	Lake Mead National Recreation Area
LVWD	Las Vegas Valley Water District
NPS	National Park Service
NRA	National Recreation Area
ORRRC	Outdoor Recreation Resources Review Commission
PWA	Public Works Administration
PWC	Personal Watercraft
SNWA	Southern Nevada Water Authority
TWA	Trans World Airlines
USBR	United States Bureau of Reclamation
USGS	U.S. Geological Survey
WPB	War Production Board

Preface

It is somewhat ironic that I have lived much of my adult life in the desert. I have always felt most at ease nearest water, and certainly it has defined my outdoor recreational habits. As a child, I spent countless hours exploring the waters of Alabama and Florida with fishing rod in hand and grand expectations in mind. The type of water never mattered to me. Be it a large reservoir, free-flowing river, or natural lake, I was happy to fish wherever my dad or grandfather took me. They taught me the sport and to love the water. I still do, and I thank them for it. Those were good times.

I never realized how much those waters meant to me until I moved to the American Southwest as a young man. The old adage that absence makes the heart grow fonder certainly applied in this case. Although I found the southern Nevada desert cool (figuratively speaking), its scarcity of water and lack of fishing opportunities left me with a sense of loss.

Then, a few years after moving to Las Vegas, I discovered the great fishing to be had in the waters of Lake Mead. Certainly, as a student of history, I knew of Hoover Dam, its iconic status, its tremendous influence on the Southwest, and its place in American history, but I had never really considered the recreational opportunities its reservoir created. There, I found both world-class fishing and a history that was equally thrilling. Those waters formed the nation's largest man-made reservoir and its first National Recreation Area. This was a beautifully strange and contradictory place where water met desert and the National Park Service embraced reservoir-based recreation in an arid land. In some ways, the lake resembled its nearby urban neighbor Las Vegas. Both, environmentally speaking, really shouldn't be there. Yet, there they are. Each year, they offer millions of people exceptional places to play. Both places make people happy. Both places, with their crowds, promise, and problems, make me think about our modern expectations of and relationship with nature.

Today, an ocean away and many years removed from my youth, southern Nevada, and my first experiences on Lake Mead, I sit and ponder the long and crooked path of this book's creation. As the memories flood in, I am overwhelmed by the help I have received from those who, in most instances, bore no responsibility to offer advice, guidance, or even a listening ear. I am reminded of something profound and utterly accurate that Elliot West once wrote: "Like most historians, I am a chronic debtor." In my opinion, no better description exists of the historian. This book, like all works of history, is the product of many people's generosity. To them I owe a great debt.

First on my list of creditors is David Wrobel. He made this project available to me when I most needed it. David is an amazing scholar and mentor. I am lucky to count him among my friends.

The current editors and staff at the University of Nevada Press also proved central to making this project a reality. This book has benefited greatly from the patience of Justin Race, Matt Becker, Virginia Fontana, and Caddie Dufurrena. Likewise, series editor Char Miller and the anonymous readers who evaluated the ever-evolving manuscript provided expert suggestions throughout the entire process. It has been a true pleasure to work with everyone at the press.

The staffs of numerous libraries, historical societies, and government agencies provided expert assistance with research. Of particular note, Su Kim Chung and Delores Brownlee of UNLV's Special Collections, Lynne MacDonald and Jeannette Davis of the U.S. Bureau of Reclamation, Wade Myers of the National Park Service, and Gregory Walz of the Utah Historical Society Archives were tremendously helpful regarding the location and usage of historical documents and photographs. Likewise, the National Park Service's David Louter, along with Steve Daron and Rosie Pepito at the Lake Mead National Recreation Area, provided me with extraordinary help and feedback throughout the early stages of my research.

I wish also to acknowledge the many friends, colleagues, and associates who provided helpful advice, suggestions, and support along the way—even if sometimes indirectly and unknowingly. Each of our many conversations contributed to this book's completion and made it better. Specifically, the various scholars who worked on the Lake Mead National Recreation Area Historic Resource Study at UNLV made this book possible. These include, but are not limited to, Charles Dietrich, David Sproul, and the late Hal Rothman. Of particular note, Cindy Ott has my gratitude for her contributions to the study's periodization, topics, and chapter titles. Finally, I would be remiss if I failed to single out U.S. Forest Service Chief Historian Lincoln Bramwell's extraordinary work on the resource study. That project, and by association this book, certainly benefited from his conceptualization of area's history and his skills as a researcher and writer. I am also thankful for the editing talent of Susan Snowden and Jeff Grathwohl.

None of the preceding acknowledgments would be necessary, however, if not for the support of those closest to me. I would not have been interested in this book's topic if not for my father Lavon and grandfather Butch having introduced me early and often to fishing. I am also grateful to my mother Kaye for cultivating a child's inquisitive nature, sparking what became a lifelong appreciation of learning. My parents-in-law Sissel and Rolf also have my gratitude for allowing me the privilege of a quiet and inspiring place to write during those beautiful summers in Norway.

I am, however, most grateful for the patience and understanding of my lovely wife Marianne. Her support has been unwavering and her suggestions always spot on. I would be lost without her. Finally, I should also thank my two daughters. Nora and Sadie are the inspiration and joy that spark my creative impulse. They have spent far too much time waiting while daddy worked. I think I'll take them fishing.

Jonathan Foster

Bergen, Norway, August 8, 2015

Lake Mead
National Recreation Area

Introduction
Pacesetter in the Desert

Historian Donald Worster has described parts of the modern American West as a hydraulic society. Such a society is, he explains, "a social order based on the intensive, large-scale manipulation of water and its products in an arid setting." To a great extent, those who manipulate and control the water in such a society exercise much power and influence over the trajectory of the region and the behaviors of its people.[1]

Worster is correct that water has played an important role in the West's development, characteristics, and power relationships. From Hetch Hetchy to Owens Valley to Las Vegas, the manipulation of water has mattered. Those who control its availability and use, whether federal government or local water authorities, wield significant power in an arid landscape.

In 1936, the National Park Service (NPS) increased its role in this hydraulic society. That year, after lengthy discussions with the Bureau of Reclamation (USBR), the NPS assumed management responsibility for the throngs of recreational tourists who were converging upon the new reservoir created by Boulder Dam. Increased recreational opportunity was a product of the river's manipulation and transformation into the world's largest reservoir. Proponents of NPS control over the area argued that the service, with its two decades of experience overseeing tourism at national parks, was better suited for such a task than the Bureau. With the NPS shouldering the load of recreation management, USBR engineers could focus on overseeing the dam itself, making sure that copious amounts of electricity were generated and that water was distributed to the region's arid lands. Thus, through an interagency agreement that spelled out these roles, the NPS and USBR created the nation's first national recreation area (NRA).[2]

The creation of the Boulder Dam and the Boulder Dam Recreation Area (BDRA; later renamed the Lake Mead National Recreation Area or LMNRA) was innovative and benefited millions of Americans in the following decades. While inhabitants of the Southwest gained millions of acre-feet of water for irrigation and drinking, along with abundant electricity for industrialization and development, one must also list recreation alongside these more commonly acknowledged products of the dam. The dam's reservoir offered easily accessible, mass-scale, water-based recreation to the population of a desert environment. Millions of residents subsequently availed themselves of previously unavailable recreational activities in the years that followed.[3] The desert reservoir's extravagant offering of seemingly unlimited water-based fun became an important aspect of the "managed oasis" lifestyle that made the hydraulic society of the Southwest palatable.[4]

Yet by agreeing to manage the Boulder Dam Recreation Area, the NPS accepted both power and responsibility in terms of overseeing this oasis lifestyle. I contend that in the long term this was a bad move. Embracing such a role, the NPS placed itself in what must ultimately become an impossible situation: an obligation to reconcile the irreconcilable.

In an era when recreation has become ever more frequently viewed as a right, the interests of the recreational public in LMNRA have become pitted against an arid region's water needs and increasing emphasis on cultural and environmental preservation. It is here, with the NPS stuck in the middle, that a significant weakness of the hydraulic society becomes apparent. There simply is not enough water to satisfy all and maintain the full oasis lifestyle. Continued growth and demand, which is created by the very manipulation of the water that is at the foundation of the society, will require ever more severe regulation of water's use. As this occurs at multiple-use locations, such as arid region national recreation areas, the power of the state over personal behavior becomes ever more apparent and controversial. Some of the extravagant trappings of the oasis lifestyle, such as recreational accessibility, must be curtailed. With such difficult choices, the hydraulic society becomes less palatable. To some degree, as illustrated by the history of LMNRA, that is already happening.

In LMNRA the interests of recreationists, the wider public, and the NPS have often proved diametrically opposed. The trend seems to be increasing as recreational demand, water demand, and preservationist beliefs have all surged in recent decades. Further, the NPS management style, insufficient congressional support, and the recreation area's placement in a rapidly urbanizing area have made an already challenging situation exponentially more difficult. This leaves the NPS occupying a seemingly untenable middle ground heading into the future. Gaining a better understanding of the characteristics and consequences of this historical process is of great value for navigating a future that will likely see even greater demand for water-based recreation, even as restrictions on southwestern reservoir waters grow ever more stringent.

Historical examination of LMNRA brings this process into stark relief. Through the development and operation of LMNRA, the NPS defined NRAs in terms of relatively free and unregulated outdoor recreation. The NPS, the USBR, and private industry associated with recreational pursuits proved very effective in setting such expectations. Over the years, the extent of the local public's recreationist attitude concerning the reservoir has been evident. Locals not associated with government have consistently reacted passionately in the face of increased regulation and decreased access to their recreational activities within the area. While the iconic Hoover Dam is recognized popularly on a national scale, and associated with reclamation and its undertakings, the millions of individuals who use the area surrounding it each year experience it and perceive it in terms of fishing, hiking, swimming, and boating.

At the same time, the reservoir exists because of its water storage capacity and electricity generation. Without Lake Mead and other reservoirs that followed its path, much of the southwestern urbanization and population growth of the twentieth century could not have occurred. In this regard, the dam and its reservoir, without which there would be no recreation area, are vital national interests. While millions of visitors and locals perceive the reservoir as recreational opportunity, tens of millions depend on it for the water that sustains life and the electricity that allows livelihood. It is a centerpiece of the hydraulic society.

In a vicious cycle, usage of reservoir-based recreational areas, like the one at Lake Mead, has increased alongside the southwestern urban growth that the reservoirs' existence fostered. The more successful that reservoirs were in spurring development and population growth, the more demand arose for reservoir-based recreation areas. By the early twenty-first century, it is apparent that such a system cannot be sustained indefinitely: heavy demand, the reservoir's strategic importance, and other contextual issues have all combined with drought to overwhelm NRA resources and require more rigorous limitations on recreational activities and access. While necessary, this has not been a popular process in the minds of many Americans who expect free and unencumbered access to recreation in reservoir-based NRAs.

Water historian and legal scholar Robert Glennon once wrote "most Americans take water for granted."[5] Although he was referring to the availability and accessibility of safe drinking water, the same point could be made concerning recreational water. At LMNRA[6] this tendency to take the extravagance of water-based recreation in the desert for granted has been the result of shifting American ideas, decades of governmental intervention, and the NPS's recreational area management practices since 1936.

Prior to the creation of the recreation area, Americans' ideas regarding this portion of the Colorado River and its worth shifted to a remarkable degree. Governmental actions such as protecting wagon trains, safeguarding trade routes and mineral deposits, dispossessing Native Americans of land, and dam building all influenced and reflected the nation's values, along with what was perceived as the basis of the area's worth. Between the mid-eighteenth to early twentieth century, the region and its river's perceived basis of desirability transitioned several times from homeland to strategic transportation route to water source.

Then, as the reservoir filled behind Boulder Dam, the area became primarily a recreational destination for many Americans. Yes, it is true that its water supply and the electricity it produced probably played a more daily role in their lives. But people were separated from direct interaction with those production processes. While in their homes and turning on the tap or eating crops irrigated by the reservoir's water, the connection to the reservoir was not so obvious as it was when fishing, boating, or swimming in its waters. For the eventual 400 million recreationists who have visited the area between 1936 and 2015, the reservation became a place to play.[7]

Throughout the first several decades of the recreation area's existence, this play was free with relatively unlimited access and usage. NPS management during this era focused primarily on providing amenities and welcoming recreationists. Though there were normal safety-oriented regulations on behavior, denial of access or strict limitation of recreational activities was largely nonexistent. Until the early 2000s, the NPS did not even require entrance or usage fees at LMNRA.[8] At Lake Mead this resulted in a generational expectation of free and largely unregulated outdoor recreational behavior. Reservoir-based recreation was cheap, open, readily accessible, and people took it for granted.

Eventually, changing contextual issues such as population growth, the popularization of more varied recreation practices, increased environmental awareness, and shifting environmental conditions intervened to force the NPS to take a more active and intervening role in the recreation area. But by this time, recreationists' expectations had long been set in regard to NRAs. Subsequent attempts to limit access and regulate behavior have run counter to belief in free and unimpeded use among various population segments. This has resulted in much tension and presents a serious challenge for NPS-managed recreation areas in the twenty-first century, as circumstances require ever more regulation of activity in the recreation area.

The lessons offered by LMNRA's history are important, as it has been a pacesetter for what is today a system of NRAs. The majority of NPS-controlled NRAs, much like LMNRA, are based on the existence of large-scale reservoirs, sometimes in marginal environments.[9] Likewise, recreational demands on NRAs are likely to increase as American urban populations grow and water-based recreation becomes more and more popular.[10] At the same time, the availability of reservoir-based recreation areas is not likely to grow in tandem. Like the water in some desert reservoirs, the political will necessary to create additional large-scale reservoirs is vanishing. Environmental impact and popular-political opposition to dam building has rendered the creation of large numbers of new reservoir-based NRAs unlikely.[11] Instead, the present trend is toward dam removal to restore free-flowing rivers.[12] In some ways such monumental structures as the Hoover and Glen Canyon dams that have provided so much in the way of recreational opportunity are now artifacts of a different era and mentality. Truth be told, prolonged drought and climate change seem to call into question even their survival.

If recent history has any predictive value, it is a safe bet that future visitors will find the existing NRAs even more crowded, contested, and environmentally degraded. In turn, visitors will necessarily encounter more limitations on their recreational behavior. LMNRA, as a carryover from an earlier era when many regarded dam building as progress, has been the frontline between recreationists' demands, the environment's limitations, and the NPS's abilities. In order to best address present and future challenges regarding NRA usage, it is of vital importance that we understand the history of this first NRA. Its story has much to offer in terms of understanding precedent and for navigating the recreationist future in the hydraulic society.

Prior to the 1930s, few could have imagined the rugged Black Canyon of the Colorado River as the location of such a significant site in American history. Fewer still could have envisioned millions of people visiting the area each year in search of outdoor recreational activities that they increasingly viewed as a right of citizenship. Yet that is precisely what happened in this hard and forbidding desert chasm. As unlikely as it might have seemed, Black Canyon became home to the largest dam, largest man-made lake, and the first NRA in the United States. As such, it is a site of major historical significance. At once, LMNRA became one of the most popular recreational destinations in the world and a pacesetter in terms of federal recreational organization and management. Today there are eighteen NRAs managed by the NPS. Twelve of these have large-scale reservoirs as centerpieces.[13] Along with numerous other NRAs under the United States Forest Service's (USFS) management, all such reservoirs owe their existence to LMNRA's creation some eighty years ago.

When created, the recreation area offered people a welcoming place to play in the water in the midst of one of the nation's driest areas.[14] Approximately 300,000 Americans took the NPS up on this offer during the area's first year of existence. Eventually LMNRA annual visitation peaked in the mid-1990s, with approximately nine million people per year partaking of its recreational offerings. Although declining somewhat, recreational use has remained very heavy into the twenty-first century, typically falling between seven and eight million visits per year.[15]

The heavy usage of LMNRA was not an anomaly. As other NRAs appeared, they too encountered significant demand. By 2012, NPS-managed NRAs across the nation hosted some 44,679,478 recreationists annually. That breaks down to 2,482,193.2 visitors per national recreation area each year. This number easily surpassed the national parks' average of 1,103,453.6 visitors per park. Americans of the early twenty-first century obviously love their recreation.[16] More specifically, they love water-based recreation. Studies indicate that American participation in water-based recreation activities such as motorboating and swimming in lakes is increasing at a much faster rate than the overall population.[17] Throughout this period, it is safe to say that the primary value of the reservoir, at least in the minds of millions of Americans, was the recreational use of its water.

The recreation area that started all of this occupies an immense spatial territory of some 1.5 million acres. From its northernmost point on the Virgin River near Overton, Nevada, park boundaries run southward approximately ninety-five miles to Laughlin, Nevada. On the northeast, it borders

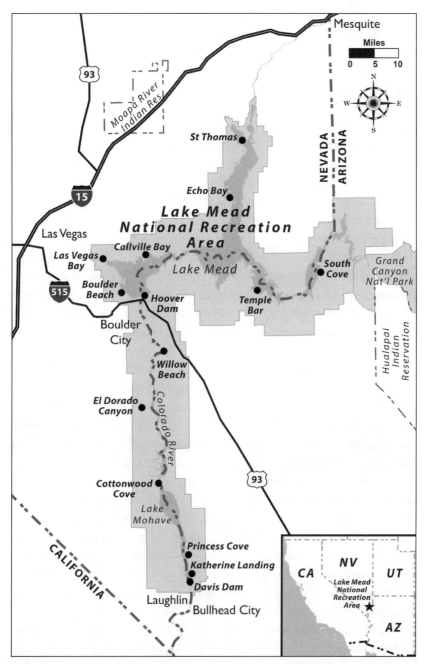

FIGURE I.1. This map of Lake Mead National Recreation Area reveals the area's large size. Courtesy of National Park Service.

Grand Canyon National Park and includes a section of the Arizona Strip north of the Colorado River. On its northwestern edge, one finds Boulder City and then, a few miles west, the heavily populated sprawl of Henderson and Las Vegas. All along its impressive north-to-south expanse, LMNRA includes several miles of territory on both sides of the Colorado River in Arizona and Nevada. In total, LMNRA encompasses an area slightly larger than the state of Delaware.

Within its boundaries lies Lake Mead, presently the largest man-made reservoir in the United States and, at one time, the world. Held back by Hoover Dam, the lake stretches some 115 miles and sits at an elevation of 1,229 feet when at full pool.[18] To the south of Lake Mead, the recreation area also includes Lake Mohave. This reservoir, a 67-mile-long expanse of water, is four miles wide at its widest point, just south of Cottonwood Cove. The proximity of both bodies of water to population centers in southern Nevada, California, and Arizona has made them popular recreational destinations for nearby urban residents and tourists seeking a break from the congestion of Los Angeles and Phoenix or the shows and casinos of Las Vegas.

The recreation area's extreme environmental setting has contributed to both its popularity and to the challenges it has faced. LMNRA is located squarely within the Mojave Desert, one of the most unforgiving and extreme environments in North America. Although geographically it is the smallest of the four desert regions of the United States, the Mojave makes up for what it lacks in size with intensity. It is the driest, hottest, and arguably most rugged of its three U.S. siblings. This land of extremes has recorded the world's second highest temperature—134 degrees Fahrenheit—at Death Valley. Average annual rainfall amounts vary between an arid 5 inches in its westernmost reaches to just 1.5 inches in some eastern areas. With such low levels of rainfall, episodes of precipitation can be astonishingly infrequent. Baghdad, California, located within the desert's southwest quadrant, holds the U.S. record for the longest period without rainfall: 767 days.[19] Historically, activity in this area has revolved around steady access to dependable water supplies. Power and survival have coincided with control of that resource.

Like the climate, the topography of the Mojave and LMNRA is characterized by extremes. While 75 percent of the desert is located between 2,000 and 4,000 feet elevation, a full 550 square miles of Death Valley plunges below sea level. At its low point of 282 feet below sea level, Death Valley

FIGURE I.2. Lake Mead's blue waters contrast with the recreation area's arid and rugged landscape, 2010. Photo by author.

claims the title of the lowest natural point in the entire western hemisphere.[20] Within LMNRA itself, elevations range from a low of 512 feet at Davis Dam to 7,072 feet at Mt. Dellenbaugh on the Arizona Strip's Shivwits Plateau. All along the river, the rugged topography is further reinforced by canyon walls and peaks that often enclose it, as if designed to thwart travel, trade, and settlement.[21]

Beyond the canyon walls, the Mojave Desert exhibits numerous north-to-south mountain ranges with intervening arid, flat valleys. Although rugged and hot, the area certainly is not devoid of life. Vegetation, consisting of the creosote bush, the Joshua tree, the burro bush, and various cacti, can be found in abundance depending on location. Also, bighorn sheep, burros, mountain lions, snakes, lizards, various birds, and desert tortoises, among other animals and insects, inhabit the desert setting.[22] On occasion their populations have grown large enough to require controversial control actions by the NPS and Bureau of Land Management.

The eastern basin of the Colorado River offers perhaps the greatest visual contrast available in the Mojave. Here, the river, winding its way through its distinctly dry desert setting, becomes a study in opposites. It is the fluid of life, once rushing wild and swelling with floods originating in the Rocky Mountains, now placidly impounded and evaporating in the desert sun. It is blue against brown, life seemingly transposed against death. This water is the engine of the history that has defined the area.

It is also important to note that the recreation area was created in very close proximity to a developing urban area. Las Vegas, which was merely a small desert town in the 1930s, had grown exponentially by the century's end. Oftentimes, in the latter decades of the twentieth century, it ranked among the fastest growing U.S. cities. Much of this growth can be credited to the existence of Hoover Dam and its reservoir. The growth itself likewise contributed to the pressures on the recreation area and its management.

The relationship of LMNRA to urban population centers did not go unnoticed. In its Policy on the Establishment and Administration of Recreation Areas of 1963, the U.S. government granted official status to national recreation areas and established the criteria they would have to meet to be designated as such. These criteria specifically required that future recreation areas be created within "easy driving distance" of urban areas.[23] This made sense, as the relationship with Las Vegas had been a positive one up until then. The city, though growing, had yet to experience the phenomenal expansion of the late twentieth century and emergence as a major American metropolis. As this occurred, the urban influence on LMNRA became more complex. For example, the spillover of urban-related crime into LMNRA endangered visitors and taxed already insufficient funding and seems to have been largely unanticipated.

On the other hand, LMNRA's proximity has certainly enriched the recreational lives of urban residents, as shown by visitation numbers. By the early twenty-first century, LMNRA ranked fifth among NPS units and second among NRAs in annual visits, placing it ahead of such beloved national parks as Grand Canyon, Yosemite, and Yellowstone. In fact, the only *national park* to outdraw LMNRA in 2012 was Great Smoky Mountains. The only *recreation area* with more visitors than LMNRA was the sprawling, discontinuous, and even more urban Golden Gate National Recreation Area.[24] And LMNRA's popularity in 2012 was no fluke. LMNRA has consistently ranked among the top five most-visited NPS units since statistics on such things have been compiled. It ranked outside the top five in annual visitation only once in the preceding twenty-year period.[25]

Such popularity was likely unanticipated when the USBR and NPS formed the Boulder Dam Recreational Area in 1936. That action, nevertheless, marked an innovative departure from traditional park service policy. For the first time, the NPS agreed to recognize and administer a national playground of sorts defined by human construction. In this initial case, the landscape's recreational value resulted primarily from construction of the dam and its reservoir. By inventing the category of national recreation area, the NPS and USBR allowed millions to enjoy the recreational aspects offered by a transformed landscape. Yet it also fostered the development of Americans' inclination to base their water-related recreational activities on the existence of nearby large-scale reservoirs. As the decades of the twentieth century passed, this became the only conceptualization of such recreation and reservoir usage that many had ever known. The public's idea of recreation and the recreational landscape thus changed with the creation of the reservoir and the NPS's acceptance of its management.

By partnering with the USBR and assuming responsibility for reservoir-based NRAs, the NPS also entered into a devil's bargain of sorts. To some degree it gave up the high ground in its opposition to dam building. On another level, it signaled its approval of outdoor recreation around large-scale, environmentally transformative structures. This acknowledgment via its cooperation with the USBR likely contributed to the bureau's future readiness to proceed with controversial reclamation projects such as Echo Park and Glen Canyon.[26]

Marc Reisner wrote in *Cadillac Desert* that had it not been for the "messianic" efforts of such reclamation, the West as we know it today would not exist. In the West's marginal environment, the existence of cities, towns, and farms depends on the dams and concrete waterways that control the water. Without such structures, areas of the West that now house millions would support only thousands. In this way, reclamation created the illusion of plenty in a land of scarcity.[27] The same can be said for reclamation's influence on recreation in the West. Large reservoirs like Lake Mead allowed for the illusion of permanent and unfettered water-based recreation in a desert. Yet as decades have passed, the fallacy of that idea has been made apparent. This, to say the least, has become problematic for a twenty-first century NPS charged with meeting the public's mid-twentieth-century concept of reservoir-based recreation.

LMNRA thus offers a lesson in the unintended consequences and complexities of humankind's attempted domination over nature that has so often accompanied outdoor recreational development and management. Isaac Newton, great Enlightenment thinker that he was, famously wrote that "for every action there is an equal and opposite reaction." Newton's third law of motion, as the phrase became known, neatly explains the interaction of force and objects in the natural world according to physics. However, when humans enter the equation, things become a bit more complicated and a lot less predictable. A more suitable natural law for human interactions might read "for every human action, there are, more often than not, unanticipated and disproportionate reactions and consequences."[28] Such has certainly been the case in regard to the eventful history of LMNRA and that fateful decision by NPS leadership to assume its management.

Yet this history is not merely the story of the NPS and LMNRA. It is alternately a history of human interaction with the natural and built environment, a history of ideas and action, and, perhaps most significantly, a history of recreational ideas. For, if anything, the story of LMNRA shows the important role that outdoor recreational activity has assumed in the lives of the people and in the halls of government during the twentieth century. How people play and approach the areas in which they play might well provide insight into what they hold important. It is, after all, what they choose do with that most valuable commodity known as time off.

This book addresses the history of the area and the recreation that has occurred within it in a chronological and primarily narrative framework. Chapters One and Two explore the foundations and historical context necessary for the development of the nation's first NRA. These chapters, spanning the period from pre-European contact to 1936, address both the historical events and shifting perceptions concerning the environment, its people, and how they valued the land's resources. It is, at once, a story of conquest, innovation, and shifting societal values and sets the stage for the eventual development and challenges faced by the first NRA.

Chapter Three examines the solidification of NPS control over the recreation area from the 1930s through the 1960s and the popularization of recreation in the area. During this era the NPS also increased the area's size and focused on improving recreational amenities for the visiting public. Also, its management practices helped set the public's expectation of free and largely unregulated recreation at LMNRA.

Chapter Four highlights the emergence of serious management complexities and challenges facing the NPS and LMNRA over the last four decades of the twentieth century. During this extraordinarily active era, conflicting priorities of various groups, ever-increasing usage, changing contextual characteristics, and newly popularized attitudes toward the environment all challenged the NPS's ability to effectively meet the public's recreational desires.

Chapter Five follows these themes into the twenty-first century but also uncovers new challenges piled on to the already difficult situation. During the first fifteen years of the new century, changing environmental characteristics and security concerns interjected themselves into the NPS management equation in dramatic fashion, further testing the ability of the NPS to effectively meet the public's recreational expectations.

All of the chapters address the relationship of government and people with the built and natural environment. At its most basic, the history of LMNRA is the story of people interacting with a marginal landscape and its water. But it is also much more. In addition to the history of how people play and how that has changed, this is the story of how various groups have interacted with each other relative to recreational behavior and setting—and how government action has shaped these interactions and expectations. In the latter regard, it is the story of water-based power over behavior in an arid land.

NOTES

1. Donald Worster, *Rivers of Empire: Water, Aridity, and the Growth of the American West* (New York: Oxford University Press, 1985), 7; Karl A. Wittfogel, *Oriental Despotism: A Comparative Study of Total Power* (New Haven: Yale University Press,), passim; also Worster, "Hydraulic Society in California," and "Hoover Dam: A Study in Domination," in *Under Western Skies: Nature and History in the American West* (New York: Oxford University Press, 1992), 53–78.

2. "Memorandum of Agreement Between the National Park Service and the Bureau of Reclamation. Relating to the Development and Administration of the Boulder Canyon Project Area," 29 August 1936, 1. Lake Mead National Recreation Area Folder, Boulder City/Hoover Dam Museum, Boulder City, Nevada. (Hereafter, "Memorandum of Agreement," 29 August 1936.) As Richard West Sellers points out, the NPS's creation of the recreation area designation was in line with New Deal emphasis on expanding national park system use and accessibility. This move, Sellers argues, also marked a turning point at which the NPS "sidestepped" its obligation to preserve land unimpaired in favor of increasing its role in recreational management.

See Richard West Sellers, *Nature in the National Parks: A History* (New Haven: Yale University Press, 1997), 132–38. It should be recognized that the National Park Service was already engaged in western reservoir management by the time of this agreement. Of particular note, reservoirs existed in Yosemite (Hetch Hetchy) and Glacier (Lake Sherburne) national parks. However, the Boulder Dam Recreation Area was the first instance of an NPS unit's establishment based on the existence of a man-made reservoir and the desire to manage its recreational usage.

3. In 1940, the combined population of states ultimately allotted Colorado River water by the Colorado River Compact (Arizona, California, Colorado, Nevada, New Mexico, Utah, Wyoming) was 9,972,000. By 2010, the combined population of the same states had increased almost sixfold to 56,762,410. In 1940, the BDNRA hosted 655,910 recreational visits. By 2014, that number had increased tenfold to 6,942,873. Bureau of the Census, "Historical Statistics of the United States, Colonial Times to 1970: Part 1" (Washington, D.C.: Department of Commerce, 1975), 24–25, 31–32, 35, 37; Paul Mackun and Steven Wilson, "Population Distribution and Change, 2000–2010" (Washington, D.C.: Department of Commerce, 2011), 2; National Park Service, "Lake Mead NRA," https://irma.nps.gov/Stats/SSRSReports/Park Specific Reports/Annual Park Recreation Visitation (1904 - Last Calendar Year)?Park=LAKE cite NRA usage by 2015.

4. Worster, *Rivers of Empire*, 330.

5. Robert Glennon, et al., "Turning on the Tap: The World's Water Problems," *Frontiers in Ecology and the Environment* 3 (November 2005):503; Robert Glennon, *Water Follies: Groundwater Pumping and the Fate of America's Fresh Waters* (Washington, D.C.: Island Press, 2002), 14.

6. In 1947, the Boulder Canyon Recreation Area's name was officially changed to the Lake Mead National Recreation Area. In the hope of avoiding confusion, I will employ the acronym LMRNA when discussing the recreation area both prior to and after 1947.

7. National Park Service, "Annual Park Recreation Visitation," https://irma.nps .gov/Stats/SSRSReports/Park%20Specific%20Reports/Annual%20Park%20Rec reation%20Visitation%20%281904%20-%20Last%20Calendar%20Year%29?Park= LAKE (accessed February 10, 2015).

8. Keith Rogers, "Lake Mead Fee Collection Figures Show High Number of $5 Passes Sold," *Las Vegas Review-Journal*, 4 June 2001.

9. The National Park Service manages eighteen national recreation areas. Of these, thirteen are based on large dams and reservoirs. Of the thirteen, ten are west of the 100th meridian.

10. H. Ken Cordell and Gregory R. Super, "Trends in Americans' Outdoor Recreation," in William C. Gartner and David W. Lime, eds., *Trends in Outdoor Recreation, Leisure, and Tourism* (Wallingford, UK: CABI Publishing, 2000), 134–35.

11. Robert Glennon, *Unquenchable: America's Water Crisis and What To Do About It* (Washington, D.C.: Island Press, 2009), 19.

12. Glennon et al., "Turning on the Tap," 503. Glennon points out that since 1999, 140 dams have been removed in the U.S. in the interest of restoring free-flowing rivers. See also the exceptional 2014 documentary *DamNation*.

13. National Park Service, "Annual Recreation Visitation by Park Type or Region for: 2014 By Park Type," https://irma.nps.gov/Stats/SSRSReports/National%20Reports /Annual%20Recreation%20Visitation%20Report%20by%20Park%20Type%20or%20 Region%20%281979%20-%20Last%20Calendar%20Year%29 (accessed February 12, 2015).

14. Diane Raines Ward, *Water Wars: Drought, Flood, Folly, and the Politics of Thirst* (New York: Penguin, 2002), 67. The area in which LMNRA is located receives about 3.8 inches of rainfall per year. This is comparable to such arid areas as Riyadh, Saudi Arabia, and Villa Cisneros in the Western Sahara.

15. National Park Service, "Annual Park Recreation Visitation," https://irma.nps .gov/Stats/SSRSReports/Park%20Specific%20Reports/Annual%20Park%20Recrea tion%20Visitation%20%281904%20-%20Last%20Calendar%20Year%29?Park=LAKE (accessed February 10, 2015).

16. Ibid.

17. Cordell and Super, "Trends in Americans' Outdoor Recreation," 135.

18. Mike Belshaw and Ed Peplow Jr., *Historic Resources Study: Lake Mead National Recreation Area, Nevada* (Denver: National Park Service, 1980), 7.

19. Peggy Larson and Lane Larson, *The Deserts of the Southwest: A Sierra Club Naturalist's Guide*, 2nd ed. (San Francisco: Sierra Club Books, 1997), 88.

20. Ibid., 87–89; Edmund C. Jaeger, *The North American Deserts* (Stanford: Stanford University Press, 1957), 123–125.

21. Belshaw and Peplow, *Historic Resources Study*, 7. Mt. Dellenbaugh and the accompanying Shivwits Plateau were included in the Grand Canyon–Parashant National Monument at its creation by presidential proclamation 7265 on January 11, 2000. "Grand Canyon-Parashant National Monument: Records of Decision and Resource Management Plan/General Management Plan," Bureau of Land Management/National Park Service, February 2008, 1.

22. Jaeger, *North American Desert*, 126.

23. Recreation Advisory Council. "Federal Executive Branch Policy Governing the Selection, Establishment, and Administration of National Recreational Areas," March 26, 1963, in Lary M. Dilsaver, ed., *America's National Parks: The Critical Documents* (New York: Rowman & Littlefield, 1994).

24. National Park Service, "Annual Park Ranking Report for Recreation Visitors in 2012," https://irma.nps.gov/Stats/SSRSReports/National%20Reports/Annual%20 Park%20Ranking%20Report%20%281979%20-%20Last%20Calendar%20Year%29 (accessed February 22, 2016). The top five NPS areas ranked according to visitation for 2012 were: 1) Blue Ridge Parkway, 2) Golden Gate NRA, 3) Great Smoky Mountains NP, 4) George Washington Memorial Parkway, and 5) Lake Mead NRA. For statistics concerning nonrecreational visits, see: National Park Service, "Annual Park

Ranking Report for NonRecreation Visitors in: 2012," https://irma.nps.gov/Stats /SSRSReports/National%20Reports/Annual%20Park%20Ranking%20Report%20 %281979%20-%20Last%20Calendar%20Year%29 (accessed February 22, 2016).

25. National Park Service," Annual Park Ranking Report for Recreation Visitors in 2011," https://irma.nps.gov/Stats/SSRSReports/National%20Reports/Annual%20 Park%20Ranking%20Report%20%281979%20-%20Last%20Calendar%20Year%29 (accessed February 22, 2016). LMNRA ranked sixth in terms of visitation among NPS units for the year 2011.

26. Douglas Dodd, "Boulder Dam Recreation Area: The Bureau of Reclamation, the National Park Service, and the Origins of the National Recreation Area Concept at Lake Mead, 1929–1936," in *The Bureau of Reclamation: History Essays from the Centennial Symposium*, edited by Brit Allan Storey. Denver: U.S. Bureau of Reclamation, 2008; for discussion of the damming of Glen Canyon, see Jared Farmer, *Glen Canyon Dammed: Inventing Lake Powell and the Canyon Country* (Tucson: University of Arizona Press, 1999), passim.

27. Marc Reisner, *Cadillac Desert: The American West and Its Disappearing Water*, rev. ed. (New York: Penguin Books, 1993), 2–3.

28. Sociologist Robert K. Merton popularized a similar argument in the 1930s, now popularly known as the Law of Unintended Consequences. In his article "The Unanticipated Consequences of Purposive Social Action," Merton addressed the unavoidable nature of unintended consequences as a result of purposeful social action aimed at the reform of complex entities. This certainly holds true as well for humankind's interventionist transformation of the physical environment and organizational systems of relationships with that environment.

CHAPTER ONE

Transformations

The Middle Colorado River Area to 1900

On September 30, 1935, President Franklin D. Roosevelt looked out from Boulder Dam and surveyed the placid water that had once rushed unfettered, red and foaming, down the West's mightiest river. With triumphant enthusiasm, he proclaimed this dam "an engineering victory of the first order—another great achievement of American resourcefulness, skill and determination." America had, in the president's opinion, triumphed over nature and transformed "a cactus covered waste" into "a twentieth century marvel."[1] Yet long before a concrete dam plugged the free-flowing Colorado River and Roosevelt declared victory over nature, the area was far from a desert wasteland. Instead, it teemed with people and historical activity. And before Americans could dominate and transform the local environment, there first had to be a transformation of inhabitance and attitudes toward the land and its resources.

This transformative process began with the arrival of Europeans in the area during the seventeenth century. As in the rest of the Americas, they arrived rather late. By the 1600s humans had lived along the river for thousands of years. Native Americans, for example, were well established in the area between today's Grand Canyon National Park and Needles, California, by the time the first Spaniard showed up. Their nations included the Hualapai, Mojave, Chemehuevi, and Southern Paiute. Even these groups, which predated the Spaniards by hundreds of years, were relative newcomers when viewed against the depth of history. Over thousands of years, humans and their cultures had survived and in some cases flourished in this challenging environment. For the most part, they achieved a balance in which their numbers reflected the land's carrying capacity relative to their technology.[2]

But on the heels of European arrival, the millennia-long era of Native American preeminence along the winding, muddy waters came to a relatively abrupt halt. Within three hundred years the area and its rivers were transformed beyond recognition. Previously dominant groups were left dispossessed, dependent, and in some cases all but destroyed. In their place, a society stood that was far more interested in the "progress" and profit promised by the technological domination of nature than it was with the land's limitations. Boulder Dam, with its electricity, endless acre-feet of irrigation and drinking water, and modernistic design symbolized this society's relationship with the natural world. To them and to us, it has meant a national progress attested by the growth of southwestern cities, desert crops, and, not least of all, the first national playground.

That playground and those cities did not appear from interaction with some empty frontier void and without contest. Instead, they were the result of long and sometimes brutal interactions between groups with differing ideas concerning the best present and future use of the river and its surroundings.

When Europeans first arrived in this region of the Colorado River, they viewed it in terms of opportunity. They came as missionaries, conquistadors, and explorers intent on proselytizing, gaining wealth, and developing efficient overland routes to Spain's coastal California settlements. To them the river was alternately a passageway and a prospective source of wealth as the lifeblood for civilizations inhabiting the surrounding area. Through their actions the Spaniards began the transformation of the area that has continued to the present day. Their primary contribution to this process can be found in the opening of the area to travel. As a result of the Spaniards' activities, future generations of Mexican and American citizens enjoyed trade routes between Santa Fe and Monterrey that eventually became the Old Spanish Trail. This artery of people and commerce served as a corridor for trade and settlement well into the nineteenth century.

Don Juan de Oñate, the grandson-in-law of conquistador Hernán Cortés, holds the distinction of heading the first recorded European expedition into the area. His expedition made early contact with the area's Native American populations.[3] The party sought to open an easy trade route to the "South Sea" from the New Mexico colony Oñate established in 1598. Passing just south of the present day Laughlin, Nevada, Oñate's group came in contact with the Mojave Indians in 1604.[4] Fray Escobar, one of the Franciscan priests who accompanied the expedition, described the encounter:

The first nation of people whom we met at this river was called *Amacava*. We found them to be very friendly. They furnished us with maize, beans, and cala-bashes, which constitute the ordinary food of all the people along the river and which they grow throughout this river valley.[5]

The Mojave were also quick to indicate the existence of other populations and societies farther upriver.[6]

In 1773 the viceroy of New Spain commissioned Captain Juan Bautista de Anza to open an overland route between Sonora, the Colorado River, and settlements in California. Anza persuaded New Mexico missionary Fray Francisco Garcés to accompany the expedition because of his extensive knowledge of the region. Along the way, Garcés could also do the Church's and the king's bidding by converting any Native Americans he encountered and having them swear allegiance to the Spanish Crown.[7]

Even though the expedition found its way to the new Spanish settlements in California, Garcés was left disappointed in the expedition's religious accomplishments. Often he experienced difficulty converting Native Amer-icans to Catholicism, as the expedition lacked translators to relate his con-version message. When he succeeded in assembling a group of Native Amer-icans with whom communication was possible, he employed "his Christ on a crucifix…and canvas painted on both sides, one showing the Virgin Mary and the other a damned man," in his attempts to convert the likely curious and amused onlookers.[8]

Garcés was also dissatisfied with the route to California blazed by the Anza party. Believing it was too dangerous, he accompanied Anza on a second pathfinding expedition from Tubac to California in late 1775. This time Garcés left the Anza expedition in the vicinity of Yuma and eventually traveled upriver near what now is southern Nevada.[9] From there he trav-eled overland to the San Gabriel Mission in California. His expedition thus became the first comprised of Europeans to traverse this section of what eventually became the Old Spanish Trail.[10]

That same year, an additional party of Spanish explorers busied them-selves opening another segment of the Old Spanish Trail to the northwest. Friars Atanasio Domínguez and Silvestre Vélez de Escalante set out from Santa Fe on July 29, 1776, with the intention of finding a land route from that mission to the one at Monterrey, California. Though the expedition got lost and failed to accomplish this goal, it unwittingly established the northern fork of the Old Spanish Trail.[11]

Between the 1820s and the 1840s, the trail was defined and made profitable. Throughout these decades both Mexican and American expeditions sought furs and transported goods along the increasingly busy trail. American fur trappers, for example, entered the area beginning with the exploits of Jedediah Smith in the mid-1820s. Other expeditions soon followed, searching for untapped beaver habitats and easy transportation routes to California. These included parties led by such well-known trappers and explorers as Ewing Young, James O. Pattie, Antonio Armijo, Peter Skene Ogden, George C. Yount, William Wolfskill, and John C. Fremont.[12] Armijo's party of 1829 turned out to be particularly significant, as its success demonstrated the financial feasibility of trade over the Old Spanish Trail between New Mexico and California.[13] By the 1840s, the 1,200-mile trail proved very valuable to Mexican and American traders, soldiers, and eventually settlers as they journeyed toward California.[14]

With this increased traffic along the trail, the area served increasingly as an intersection of cultures. Native Americans, whose homelands spanned the route, often found their survival threatened. The ever-increasing numbers of travelers through the area placed unsustainable burdens on the natural resources that local peoples depended on for survival. Wagon trains of settlers and convoys of soldiers trampled, foraged, and depleted grasses and water sources key to local survival.

In particular, the development of a profitable mule trade along the Old Spanish Trail devastated Native American settlements. Traders bought large herds of mules at the California rancheros and sold them as far east as St. Louis, Missouri. In trade for mules, the New Mexicans brought Mexican serapes, Navajo blankets, other textiles, and such minerals as silver and turquoise. There was also extensive, and often illegal, trade of Indian slaves.

Even if profitable, the trip was perilous, long, and devastating. Large caravans with scores of animals and people became the norm. Traders seemed unaware of the heavy burden this placed on fragile societies and ecosystems. Out of desperation, as their limited resources disappeared, some local Indians occasionally employed violence against the caravans. Almost always, the purpose of these attacks was to procure livestock—not for transportation or status, but as food for hungry families.[15]

Beyond trappers and traders, the American military also began to intrude into the area during the 1840s. Much of this activity resulted from the creation of the United States Army Corps of Topographical Engineers in 1838. Answering directly to the President of the United States and the Secretary of War, the Corps began a systematic survey of the West with the intention of assisting U.S. expansion across the continent. John C. Fremont, the most well known of the engineers, traveled through the area in 1844. Although it was Mexican territory at this time, he took notes on the tribes and landscapes he encountered and ultimately published a well-received record of his expedition.[16] Soon thereafter, he helped bring this land under the political control of the United States through his activities during the Mexican War.

Following the acquisition of the area by the United States, as a result of that war, traffic increased significantly on the Old Spanish Trail. This traffic, along with subsequent permanent settlement in the Colorado River area, drastically influenced the local Native Americans' experience. As settler wagon trains, some numbering hundreds of wagons, passed through they placed even more pressure on the marginal environment's resources. There was growing concern over conflict between Native Americans and whites.[17] Such anxiety prompted the government to station troops at the most popular Colorado River crossing to protect westbound travelers. Justified or not, this outpost, located approximately halfway between modern-day Parker Dam and Needles, California, eventually became known as Fort Mojave.[18]

The presence of the U.S. troops was further felt in the area in the form of mapping and military expeditions. After the Mexican War, military topographical engineers received orders to organize expeditions in search of navigable rivers, wagon roads, and suitable railroad locations. This direct military intrusion added to the contested nature of the area and disrupted Native American ways of life. It also facilitated increased trade and settlement, as well as rivalries between settler groups. Notable expeditions that traversed this area of the Colorado River during the mid-nineteenth century include the Sitgreaves Expedition (1851), Whipple Expedition (1853–54), Ives Expedition (1858), Beale Expedition of 1857–58, and John Wesley Powell's journey down the Colorado River (1869). The creation and actions of these expeditions also indicate that the U.S. government recognized the strategic importance of the Colorado River. Quite simply, in addition to its water and possible mineral resources, the river offered the only water entrance and outlet for a large interior region, with potential for developing a thriving river trade. Military exploration of the river itself, such as the steamboat exploration of the Ives Expedition, promoted both U.S. control and increased river steamboat use.[19]

The U.S. government was not alone in recognizing the potential of the river as an avenue of commerce and transportation. Latter Day Saints leader Brigham Young also displayed a keen interest in establishing steam travel on the Colorado. To Young, the prospect of transportation from the Pacific, up the Colorado, then overland into Utah proper stood central to his vision of a Mormon homeland and was too tempting to ignore. He believed that control of the Colorado River was key to obtaining and maintaining Mormon self-sufficiency.[20] Such control would require the establishment of at least one successful Mormon-controlled port on the river.[21]

Young made his goals clear concerning the river at the LDS general conference of October 1864 in Salt Lake City. Here he spoke of the waterway as "another path to bring home the Saints." He also alluded to how such a port could transform nearby St. George into "an inland station for the other communities...and an outpost to furnish supplies."[22] Shortly thereafter, Young directed Bishop Anson Call to go to the Colorado River, find a suitable site, and construct a mission at the head of navigation.[23]

Call, having been told some years earlier by Mormon founder Joseph Smith that he would "do great work" in the West, "building cities from one end of that country to the other," accepted the task without hesitation.[24] On Friday, December 2, 1864, Call and a party that included famed Mormon explorer Jacob Hamblin arrived at a spot on the river "a mile below the narrows above the mouth of the Black Canyon." Here, on a rocky point above the high water line, Call determined that he had found the best location for the proposed port. Once surveyed, he named the new settlement Callville.[25] The settlement, however, never prospered in the manner Young had envisioned. Instead, difficulties in river navigation just below Callville, combined with competition from more accessible downstream ports such as Yuma and Hardyville, limited Callville's growth. The *Salt Lake City Daily Telegraph* summed up the prospective Mormon port's fate in November of 1867 by asking the rhetorical question: "Callville—where is it? Echo answers gone!"[26]

Another role intended for Callville had been as a port for the importation of farm machinery, supplies, and export of cash crops. Specifically, Brigham

FIGURE 1.1. Ruins of Callville, Nevada, in the 1920s. Used by permission, Utah State Historical Society.

Young saw the southern areas as suitable for the production of cotton, grapes, and wheat. If successful, such production could provide increased self-sufficiency and wealth for the territory. Furthermore, if the northern settlements could procure cotton from southern settlements, then it would decrease Mormon dependence on the American South or international markets. As the Civil War raged and interrupted the flow of cotton from the South, this rationale took on increased importance.[27]

In October of 1864 Young instructed some 183 individuals to go forth and settle such colonies south of St. George on the Muddy and Virgin rivers. These settlements, collectively known as the Muddy Mission, were to serve as stations along the route from the Pacific, up the Colorado River, through St. George, and on to Salt Lake. Further, they were to engage in the agricultural production of warm-weather crops and head off non-LDS encroachment. Of the Muddy Mission settlements, St. Thomas experienced the most success before eventually succumbing to the rising waters of Lake Mead in 1938.[28]

The Mormons were not the only Americans stepping up their activities during this period. In the river's El Dorado Canyon, the discovery of gold led to an influx of settlers beginning in the 1860s. The mining settlement that followed probably ranks among the West's most rough and tumble. "Lawless" was the word often used to describe this camp, which at that point claimed a population of 1,500. Despite having its own post office and heavy investment from the East, El Dorado Canyon often lacked all other

FIGURE 1.2. Aerial photograph showing Saint Thomas, Nevada, succumbing to the rising waters of Boulder Dam Reservoir, June 1938. Courtesy of the United States Bureau of Reclamation.

organizational structures, including organized law enforcement. From 1867 to 1868 the army established a garrison at the camp to provide some semblance of protection for the profitable operations.[29]

Beyond El Dorado Canyon, gold discoveries downriver at La Paz, Katherine, Gila, and Prescott also helped redefine the region in terms of mineral wealth. Further, large salt mines to the immediate north of El Dorado Canyon and the discovery of lead in Cataract Canyon added diversity to this picture. All of these factors brought more Americans to the area and resulted in tension with Native Americans.[30]

Some of the new arrivals eschewed mining for ranching along the Arizona Strip. These ranchers, like the miners to their south, encroached upon Native lands. The ranchers created hard feelings as they enlarged their herds and secured access to springs and water sources throughout the strip—often at gunpoint.[31]

In 1863, miners killed two members of the Havasupai Nation near a mine in Weaver. This touched off a decade of altercations that included a mas-

FIGURE 1.3. Steamboat traffic in the El Dorado Canyon area of the Colorado River, 1890. Used by permission, Utah State Historical Society.

sacre of Native Americans by residents of the river town Hardyville, which had been established to supply the river trade for the mining camps. By 1865, much of the area teetered on the verge of all-out war. At this point the U.S. Army intervened to secure what the government also recognized as an area of rich mineral resources. The ensuing Hualapai War of 1866 to 1868 ended only after Hualapai leader Sherum and all of his followers were forced onto a reservation near Peach Springs, Arizona.[32]

Meanwhile, in an effort to impress and thus pacify the Mojave Indians, the military sent tribal leader Irataba on a visit to Washington, D.C., in 1865. Irataba, having been received by President Lincoln and impressed by American strength, returned to the Colorado feeling that continued Mojave resistance was futile. His trip also served to help Charles D. Poston, Indian agent for the territory of Arizona, convince Washington of the need for a reservation on the Colorado River.[33]

Officials in Washington agreed with Poston, and that same year set aside some 75,000 acres surrounding Fort Mojave as a reservation. By 1867, the government had appropriated funds and begun construction on a large irrigation canal for the reservation. When completed in 1870, Irataba convinced many of the Mojave to move to its vicinity and take up farming. They did not settle completely, however, as evidenced by continued skirmishes with other local tribes. Nevertheless, significant altercations between the Americans and Mojave came to an end with the opening of the reservation.[34]

The Colorado River Reservation proved significant in the lives of the area's other Native American cultures. In 1874, the remaining Hualapai, despite having coexisted relatively peacefully with Americans and serving in large numbers in the U.S. Army as guides, were forcefully relocated to the reservation. Here, the Hualapai encountered disease, hunger, and hostility; in addition, they were employed to dig irrigation ditches. Unhappy with such circumstances, they quickly left the reservation and returned to their homeland in 1875. The same year, they were deported once more to an area on the reservation farther to the south near La Paz. Again, they fled and returned north. Eight years of intermittent violence with miners and ranchers followed, until President Chester A. Arthur ultimately created the 900,000-acre Hualapai Reservation by executive order on January 4, 1883.[35]

The federal government also attempted to place the Chemehuevi on the Colorado River Reservation following its establishment. The attempt was even less successful than previous efforts with the Hualapai. The Chemehuevi simply refused to move to a reservation located squarely in Mojave territory. By this time, strong tension existed between the two groups, as they had been at war with each other from 1865 to 1871. Direct confrontation between the Chemehuevi and the U.S. military had been limited historically to the killing of two soldiers and the occasional harassment of livestock. These events had occurred as pressure on Chemehuevi lands increased due to the establishment of U.S. mail and supply routes through their territory. Relations had otherwise been cordial, with the military regularly utilizing the Chemehuevi as scouts and trackers.[36]

Regardless, the U.S. persisted in its efforts to relocate the Chemehuevi to the Colorado River Reservation. In 1874, the government added a section to the reservation specifically for this purpose. Because of violence between the Chemehuevi and Mojave, many of whom already resided within this reservation, most of the Chemehuevi refused to relocate until the very late nineteenth and early twentieth centuries. Even then, many took refuge among the Cahuilla at Twenty-Nine Palms, California. Eventually, in 1911, these Chemehuevi entered the Morongo Reservation with the Cahuilla and in Banning.[37]

Like the Chemehuevi and the Hualapai, members of the Southern Paiute found themselves faced with the prospect of reservation confinement during the tense atmosphere of the mid-1860s. As early as 1858, Commissioner of Indian Affairs Charles E. Mix stated that the only course of action "compatible with the obligations of justice and humanity" was to place the "Indians on small reservations of land…until they could make the necessary exertions to support themselves."[38] In the years that followed, as miners entered and Mormons consolidated their settlements in the area, pressure increased on the government to remove the Southern Paiutes to reservations, albeit on a more permanent basis than the one implied by the commissioner.

By 1865, pressure had reached a critical level. In September of that year, Utah Superintendent of Indian Affairs O. H. Irish negotiated the Treaty of Spanish Fork with six supposed Paiute leaders. Despite the fact that no cultural precedent existed for them to exercise such power, the leaders agreed to give up all claim to traditional Southern Paiute lands and relocate to the Uintah Reservation in northeastern Utah. In return, their people would receive farming instruction, equipment, and supplies. But citing fear of their traditional enemies the Utes, most Paiute simply refused to abide by the treaty. In turn, the U.S. government never ratified the treaty.[39]

Five years later in 1870, the newly appointed Indian agent for southern Nevada, R. N. Fenton, recommended that the Southern Paiute be placed on a reservation to be located on the upper Muddy River some twenty to thirty miles north of St. Thomas. Here, the Paiute would be granted 700 to 1,000 acres of marginal land. Some three years later, Colorado River explorer John Wesley Powell and then-Nevada agent for the Southern Paiute, George W. Ingalls, serving as part of a special commission sent by the Commissioner of Indian Affairs, suggested alternative reservation locations on the Sevier and Paria rivers in Utah. Powell and Ingalls felt that these areas afforded greater opportunity for successful agriculture because of better soil and water availability. Yet upon reconsidering the historical animosity between the Ute and Paiute, they agreed that the tribes should be placed in the area previously suggested by Fenton.[40]

On March 7, 1873, Agent Ingalls submitted a recommendation to the U.S. Department of Interior's Office of Indian Affairs outlining the proposed reservation. His proposal called for a reservation

…commencing at a point on the north bank of the Colorado River where the eastern line of Nevada strikes the same, running thence due north with said eastern line to a point far enough north from which a line running due west will pass one mile north of Muddy Springs, running due west from said point to the 115th Meridian of west longitude, thence south with said meridian to a point due west from the place of beginning; thence due east to the west bank of the Colorado River, thence following the west and north bank of the same to the place of the beginning.[41]

Five days later, President Ulysses S. Grant set aside the described area by executive order. The president and the Department of Interior intended this newly created reservation to house "Pai Ute and other Indians" of the Colorado River area.[42] Then Powell and Ingalls, believing that the reservation lacked resources and was too small for the number of Native Americans to be located there, suggested enlargement to include additional agricultural land and timberland to the west. President Grant acted on this recommendation on February 12, 1874, redefining reservation boundaries

…beginning at a point in the middle of the Colorado River of the West eight miles east of the one hundred and fourteenth degree of West Longitude, thence due north to the 37th degree of North Latitude; thence west with said parallel to a point twenty miles west of the one hundred and fifteenth degree of West Longitude; thence due south thirty-five miles; thence due east thirty six miles; thence due south to the middle of the main channel of the Colorado River of the West; thence due south to the middle of the main channel to the place of beginning.[43]

This enlargement, by eight miles to the east and twenty miles to the west, stirred the local public's opposition to the reservation. While local whites had clamored for the removal of the Southern Paiute to a reservation, they did not envision one so large or in such close proximity. In the *Pioche Daily Record,* for example, the editor questioned why the reservation was to be placed so close to a large settlement and should include within its boundaries an area so rich in mineral wealth. In the editor's opinion, less valuable land to the south offered a much better option.[44]

By late 1874, Moapa Reservation Agent A. J. Barnes succumbed to such pressure. Barnes recommended that the Bureau of Indian Affairs remove any lands with mineral potential from reservation territory. Congress, in an effort to appease local sentiment, acted on Barnes's recommendation, first by attempting to disband the reservation completely and then by reducing its overall size from 39 square miles to 1,000 acres, or 1.6 square miles. In July 1875, following an official survey, the General Land Office of the United States recorded the greatly reduced official boundaries of the Moapa Valley Paiute Reservation. Conditions on the cramped and resource-poor reservation deteriorated steadily from that time until the turn of the twentieth century. By 1900, very few of the Colorado River's Southern Paiute remained there.[45]

After failing in its efforts to relocate Southern Paiute to the Moapa Reservation, the U.S. government, to a great degree, withdrew from similar attempts in the area throughout the 1880s and 1890s. Instead, the next round of reservation building resulted from the actions of a prominent local citizen. Anthony W. Ivins, Mormon bishop and owner of a large ranch in southwestern Utah, petitioned the government in the late 1880s for a federal appropriation to remove members of the Shivwits band of the Southern Paiute from their Arizona Strip homeland. Ivins, along with other southern Utah ranchers, believed that by removing the Paiute they could realize the true ranching potential of the Arizona Strip. After securing government approval and monetary support for this endeavor, Ivins oversaw the Shivwits' removal to a location on the Santa Clara River west of St. George. Ivins also directed the relocation of members of the Gunlock, Saint George, and Uinkaret bands to the reservation in 1891. The federal government took little interest in the reservation beyond supporting the school established by Ivins and did not declare the reservation official until 1903.[46]

By the dawn of the twentieth century, the landscape of this section of the Colorado River and the cultures that had existed there had undergone tremendous transformation. Formerly a landscape defined as home for Native Americans, it fully reflected the American hallmarks of profit-seeking and industry by 1900. Now under U.S. control, the area was no longer defined in terms of life, beliefs, and population carrying capacity, as it had been by Native Americans. It entered the new century defined by resources relative to benefit and profitability. Americans viewed it in terms of strategic value, trade, and minerals. Through this transition of place relative to ideas and action, the river had been redefined in terms of capitalistic opportunity. This early conversion of meaning and use was essential for the even greater transformation that followed over the next half-century. In the next stage of the river's existence, the government-sponsored domination of the river's water itself offered the ever-growing Industrial Age nation a seemingly grand opportunity to achieve its ideals of progress and plenty in its arid, southwestern most region. Ultimately, that plenty would include recreational enjoyment for a burgeoning population.

NOTES

1. "Colorado River Tamed Today," *Las Vegas Evening Review-Journal,* 1 February 1935; "Boulder Dam Job Completed 2 Years Ahead of Schedule," *Las Vegas Evening Review-Journal,* 20 September 1935; Ditzel, "A Dam Site: Better than an Unleashed River," *Westways* 68, November, 1976, 82–83; Franklin Roosevelt, "Boulder Dam Dedication Speech," 30 September 1935, transcript in *Vital Speeches of the Day* 2 (October 7, 1935):25.

2. Joseph A. Ezzo, *A Class I Cultural Resources Survey of the Moapa and Virgin Valley, Clark County Nevada,* Statistical Research Technical Series No. 58, Report Submitted to USDI Bureau of Reclamation Lower Colorado Region, 1996, 36–47.

3. In addition to being married to the granddaughter of Cortés, Oñate was heir to one of the largest mining fortunes in the New World. His father had established the fabulously productive silver mines at Zacatecas. At the time of his royal grant to found the New Mexico colony and thus pacify the northern frontier, Oñate was one of the wealthiest men in the realm. James E. Officer, *Hispanic Arizona, 1536–1856* (Tucson: University of Arizona Press, 1987), 27.

4. Jay J. Wagoner, *Early Arizona: Prehistory to Civil War* (Tucson: University of Arizona Press, 1975), 67; Officer, *Hispanic Arizona,* 27.

5. Kenneth M. Stewart, "The Mohave Indians of Hispanic Times," *Kiva* 22 (October 1966):28–29.

6. Wagoner, *Early Arizona,* 68.

7. Ibid., 115–18.

8. Francisco Garcés, *A Record of Travels in Arizona and California, 1775–1776,* translated and edited by John Galvin (San Francisco: John Howell Books, 1965), v–vi.

9. Francisco Garcés, *On the Trail of a Spanish Pioneer: Diary and Itinerary of Francisco Garcés in His Travels Through Sonora, Arizona, and California, 1775–1776,* translated by Elliot Coues (New York: Francis P. Harper, 1900), 219–24 (hereafter, *Garcés Diary*); Cline, *Exploring the Great Basin,* 36; Wagoner, *Early Arizona,* 129; Knack, *Boundaries Between: The Southern Paiutes, 1775–1995* (Lincoln: University of Nebraska Press, 2001), 32.

10. LeRoy R. Hafen and Ann W. Hafen, *Old Spanish Trail: Santa Fe to Los Angeles* (Glendale: Arthur H. Clark Company, 1954), 79.

11. Ibid., 71–80.

12. Robert C. Euler, "Southern Paiute Ethnohistory," *University of Utah Anthropological Papers* 78 (Salt Lake City: University of Utah Press, 1966), 37.

13. David J. Weber, *The Mexican Frontier, 1821–1846: The American Southwest Under Mexico* (Albuquerque: University of New Mexico Press, 1982), 134–35.

14. LeRoy R. Hafen and Ann W. Hafen, *Old Spanish Trail: Santa Fe to Los Angeles* (Glendale: Arthur C. Clarke Company, 1954), 19–20.

15. Weber, *The Mexican Frontier,* 134–35; United States Department of Interior, "National Historic Trail Feasibility Study and Environmental Assessment" (National Park Service, 2001), 9-10; Alley, John R. Jr., "Prelude to Dispossession: The Fur Trade's Significance for the Northern Utes and Southern Paiutes," *Utah Historical Quarterly* 50 (spring 1982):116, 118; Alice Margaret Hoffman, "The Evolution of the Highway from Salt Lake City to Los Angeles" (MA thesis, University of Southern California, 1936), 61–62.

16. Robert V. Hine and John Mack Faragher, *The American West: An Interpretive History* (New Haven: Yale University Press, 2000), 195–205; James Ronda, "Passion and Imagination in the Exploration of the American West," in William Deverell, *A Companion to the American West* (Malden, MA: Blackwell, 2004), 53–76.

17. Douglas Charles Braithwaite, "The Mastery of Cultural Contradictions: Developing Paiute Indian Leadership," PhD diss. (Massachusetts Institute of Technology, 1971), 159–160.

18. Irene J. Brennan, ed. *Fort Mojave, 1859–1890: Letters of the Commanding Officers* (Manhattan, KS: MA/AH Publishing, 1980), vii.

19. Lorenzo Sitgreaves, *Report of an Expedition down the Zuni and Colorado Rivers,* 32nd Cong., 2nd Sess., Senate Exec. Doc. 59 (Washington D.C., 1853); Hubert Bancroft, *History of Arizona and New Mexico: 1530–1888* (Albuquerque: Horn & Wallace, 1962), 481; Andrew Wallace, "Across Arizona to the Big Colorado: The Sitgreaves Expedition of 1851," *Arizona and the West* 26 (winter 1984):326, 354; A. W. Whipple, *Explorations and Surveys to Ascertain the Most Practical and Economical Route for a Railroad from the Mississippi River to the Pacific Ocean,* 33rd Cong., 2nd Sess., Senate Exec. Doc. No. 78 (Washington D.C., 1856); Grant Foreman, *A Pathfinder in the Southwest; The Itinerary of Lieutenant A. W. Whipple During his Explorations for a Railway Route from Fort Smith to Los Angeles in the Years 1853 and 1854* (University of Oklahoma Press: Norman, 1941), 232; Balduin Möllhausen, *Diary of a Journal from the Mississippi to the Coasts of the Pacific With a United States Government Expedition,* trans. Mrs. Percy Sinnett (London: Longman, Brown, Green, Longmans, & Roberts, 1858), 246; "The Pacific Railroad: Indian Tribes on Mr. Whipple's Route," *San Francisco Sun* and *New York Times,* 27 April 1854; Joseph C. Ives, *Report Upon the Colorado River of the West in 1857 and 1858,* 36th Cong., 1st Sess., Senate Ex. Doc. (Washington D.C., 1861), 21–22; David H. Miller, "The Ives Expedition Revisited: A Prussian's Impressions," *Journal of Arizona History* 13 (spring 1972), 1–25; Joseph C. Ives to Cora Semmes Ives, February 19, 1857. Joseph C. Ives Collection, Box 1, Folder 1, UNLV Special Collections; Joseph C. Ives to Cora Semmes Ives, February 11, 1857. Joseph C. Ives Collection, Box 1, Folder 1, UNLVSPC; Joseph C. Ives to Cora Semmes Ives, February 7, 1857. Joseph C. Ives Collection, Box 1, Folder 1, UNLVSPC; Joseph C. Ives to Cora Semmes Ives, February 11, 1857. Joseph C. Ives Collection, Box 1, Folder 1, UNLVSPC; Joseph C. Ives to Cora

Semmes Ives, February 19, 1857. Joseph C. Ives Collection, Box 1, Folder 1, UNLVSPC; Joseph C. Ives to Cora Semmes Ives, March 14, 1857. Joseph C. Ives Collection, Box 1, Folder 1, UNLVSPC; "The Colorado Expedition," *New York Times,* 21 July 1858; Carl Briggs and Clyde Francis Trudell, *Quarterdeck & Saddlehorn: The Story of Edward F. Beale, 1822–1893* (Glendale, CA: Arthur C. Clark Company, 1983), 187–192; Edward F. Beale, *The Report of the Superintendent of the Wagon Road from Fort Defiance to the Colorado River,* United States House of Representatives, 35th Congress, Ex. Doc No. 124, May 12, 1858.

20. Young, with knowledge of surveys at the mouth of the Colorado River, looked toward the waterway as a possible trade and immigration route to the Pacific as early as 1851. "Journal History" (Church of Jesus Christ of Latter-Day Saints Historian's Library, Salt Lake City), October 23, 1851, quoted in Melvin T. Smith, "Colorado River Exploration and the Mormon War," *Utah Historical Quarterly* 38 (summer 1970): 209, n. 9.

21. Francis H. Leavitt, "Steam Navigation on the Colorado River," *California Historical Society Quarterly* 22 (March 1943), 13. For more on Mormon trade on the Colorado River see Leonard J. Arrington, "Inland to Zion: Mormon Trade on the Colorado River, 1864-1867," *Arizona and the West* 8 (autumn 1966):239–50.

22. Brigham Young quoted in Stanley W. Paher, *Callville: Head of Navigation* (Las Vegas: Nevada Publications, undated), 5, UNLV SPC, Call# F811 C34.

23. Milton R. Hunter, "Mormons and the Colorado River," *American Historical Review* 44 (April 1939):553.

24. Anson Call, "Autobiography of Anson Call," unpublished, undated manuscript, 19. Anson Call Collection, folder 1, UNLVSPC.

25. Paher, *Callville,* 9; Leavitt, "Steam Navigation on the Colorado River," 16.

26. "Matters on the Colorado River," *Salt Lake City Daily Telegraph,* 7 December 1867.

27. Francis H. Leavitt, "Influence of the Mormon People in the Settlement of Clark County," MA thesis (Reno: University of Nevada, 1934), 68.

28. James H. McClintock, *Mormon Settlement in Arizona: A Record of Peaceful Conquest of the Desert* (Phoenix, 1921), 118; Aaron J. McArthur, "Centrally Isolated: St. Thomas, Nevada," Historic Resource Study, NPS, 2009, 21–22.

29. J. M. Townley, "Early Development of Eldorado Canyon and Searchlight Mining Districts," *Nevada Historical Society Quarterly* 11, no. 1 (spring 1968):7–17; United States Postmaster General Logbook entry, July 21, 1866. Maryellen Vallier Sandovich Collection, National Archives, 1862–1865. Box 1, folder 5. UNLVSPC; Stanley W. Paher, *Nevada Ghost Towns and Mining Camps* (Berkeley: Howell-North Books, 1970), 279–80; Dennis G. Casebier, *Camp El Dorado, Arizona Territory: Soldiers, Steamboats, and Miners on the Upper Colorado River* (Tempe: Arizona Historical Foundation, 1970), 1, 35–36, 44; "California: El Dorado Canyon," *Arizona Miner,* 18 July 1868; John L. Riggs, "The Reign of Violence in El Dorado Canyon," *Third Biennial Report of the Nevada State Historical Society* (1913):102; Pat Gallagher, "Eldorado Canyon Once Scene of Claim Jumpers, Two-Gun Killers," *Las Vegas Evening Review-Journal,* 18 March 1941.

30. Belshaw and Peplow, *Historic Resources Study,* part II, 25–32; "Rich Discovery in Arizona," *Salt Lake Weekly Tribune,* 24 April 1875; George Billingsley, "Prospector's Proving Ground: Mining and the Grand Canyon," *Journal of Arizona History* 17 (winter 1976):71.

31. Edward H. Spicer, *Cycles of Conquest: The Impact of Spain, Mexico, and the United States on the Indians of the Southwest, 1533–1960* (Tucson: University of Arizona Press, 1962), 270; Virginia Price and John T. Darby, "Preston Nutter: Utah Cattleman, 1886–1936," *Utah Historical Quarterly* 32 (summer 1964):243–45.

32. Spicer, *Cycles of Conquest,* 271; Christian W. McMillen, *Making Indian Law: The Hualapai Land Case and the Birth of Ethnohistory* (New Haven: Yale University Press, 2007), 6–7.

33. Ibid., 270.

34. Ibid., 271.

35. Ibid., McMillen, *Making Indian Law,* 14; Edgar K. Huber, "Hualapai Bay Archaeology: Class II Noncollection Cultural Resource Survey along the Eastern Arm of Lake Mead, Mohave County, Arizona." Tucson: Statistical Research Inc., 23.

36. Martha C. Knack, *Boundaries Between: The Southern Paiutes, 1775–1995* (Lincoln: University of Nebraska Press, 2001), 98–99.

37. Isabel T. Kelly and Catherine S. Fowler, "Southern Paiute," in Warren L. D'Azevedo, ed., *Handbook of North American Indians, Volume 11: Great Basin* (Washington, D.C.: Smithsonian Institution, 1983), 388.

38. Commissioner of Indian Affairs Charles Mix quoted in Knack, *Boundaries Between,* 110.

39. Kelly and Fowler, "Southern Paiute," *Handbook of North American Indians,* 11:387; Knack, *Boundaries Between,* 114–15.

40. Knack, *Boundaries Between,* 116–17.

41. Commissioner of Indian Affairs H.R. Clum to Secretary of Interior C. Delano. March 7, 1873, Sandovich Collection, Folder 2, UNLVSPC.

42. Acting Secretary of the Interior B.R. Cowen to Commissioner of Indian Affairs E.P. Smith, 14 February 1874, Sandovich Collection, Folder 2, UNLVSPC.

43. Ulysses S. Grant, Executive Order dated 12 February 1874. Sandovich Collection, Folder 2, UNLVSPC.

44. "The Threatened Outrage," *Pioche Daily Record,* 17 April 1873.

45. G.W. Ingalls, "Pai-Ute Agency, Nevada, October 1, 1874," in Commissioner of Indian Affairs Edward P. Smith, "Annual Report of the Commissioner of Indian Affairs to the Secretary of Interior for the Year 1874" (Washington: Government Printing Office, 1874), 283; Knack, *Boundaries Between,* 120; Kelly and Fowler, "Southern Paiute," *Handbook of North American Indians,* 11:388.

46. Kelly and Fowler, "Southern Paiute," *Handbook of North American Indians,* 11:389, Knack, *Boundaries Between,* 131–32, 135–37.

CHAPTER TWO

Reclamation and Recreation
The Creation of the First National Recreation Area

In *A History of Recreation: America Learns to Play,* Foster Rhea Dulles compared the growth of recreation in the United States to a river. Over time, from the 1700s to the present, American demand for recreational activities grew from a mere trickle to a raging onslaught fed by flood-swelled tributaries.[1] In light of this "onslaught," it is fitting that the Colorado River played one of the most significant roles in the history of American recreation. Yet it is also ironic that the Colorado had to be dominated and tamed in order to contribute to the raging current of twentieth-century American recreation.

During the first decades of the twentieth century, the U.S. government greatly increased its activity and influence along the Colorado. Much of this involvement can be traced to the Reclamation Act of 1902. The act paved the way for the landmark Boulder Canyon Project Act of 1928, which transformed the Colorado River and its usage. By the mid-1930s the completed Boulder Dam had tamed a previously uncontrollable waterway. Behind the dam, the world's largest reservoir glistened in the desert sun, offering life for newly irrigated fields, electricity and drinking water for growing cities, and recreational opportunity for an increasingly demanding population. In this latter capacity, domination of the river presented a challenge to its government overseers. The importance of how the government brought about and then dealt with this challenge rivals more usual discussions regarding Boulder Dam's impacts on electricity and irrigation.

The Reclamation Act of 1902 reflected American society's attitudes toward nature and thus allowed for physical domination of the river. With this act, the government claimed the capability and assumed the responsibility for transforming America's waterways in the name of progress. Quite simply, the belief was that the domination of nature through effort and technology could and would create prosperity. The landmark Boulder Canyon Project Act of 1928 carried out this mandate. Under its provisions the mighty

Colorado River ceased to flow freely to the sea. Instead, the completion of Boulder Dam in the mid-1930s tamed the river and rendered its waters available for the masses. In turn, those waters, more than the minerals near the river's banks, became the area's most valuable resource. Water could sustain crops in the countryside and populations in the cities. By turning the turbines of the world's largest hydroelectric generators, the water could also power Southwestern production and urban growth. Impounded behind the dam, the water in the world's largest reservoir also offered recreation opportunities that were impossible with a free-flowing river. As a result, this valuable resource provided for America's first federally controlled National Recreation Area.

The origins of the reclamation mindset behind this transformation can be traced to a New Orleans physician who caught gold fever in early 1849. Dr. Oliver Meredith Wozencraft, like so many Americans of his day, heeded the call of riches and set out for California. Yet between the Crescent City and the rumored gold-laden streams of the far West, Wozencraft faced a daunting and oftentimes dangerous expanse. While traversing this great distance, Wozencraft's desired destiny gave way to an environmentally determined fate. This occurred as the headstrong young doctor, contrary to the warnings of those more experienced in local travel, attempted to cross the expansive desert between the Yuma ferry of the Colorado River and the southern California coast in May. He made it as far as the Salton Sink before succumbing to heat exhaustion and falling unceremoniously from his mount. Dazed and looking out over the vast desert landscape, Wozencraft imagined a transformed environment. Suddenly the sparkle of water replaced the luster of gold as his perceived path to wealth.[2] And so began the first chapter in the story of Southwestern reclamation that would, in the century to follow, transform the Colorado, green large portions of the desert, allow for previously untenable urban growth, and place the National Park Service (NPS) squarely in the middle of a resource-versus-recreation equation.

As Wozencraft viewed the Salton Sink, he envisioned a landscape green with farms and pastures. Obviously, all that was needed to make this a reality was a steady supply of water diverted from the nearby Colorado. After he was rescued by a fellow traveler and transported back to Yuma, his idea seems to have gained some air of possibility. Locals informed him that at times of flood the river occasionally left its banks and drained through old channels into the desert toward the Salton Sink. If this was the case, then a series of canals and irrigation ditches originating at the Colorado's western bank could, without too much trouble, transform the forbidding expanse into the agricultural wonderland of his vision.

Wozencraft eventually reached California. Once there, he seemingly forgot about gold and devoted his energy to politics, medicine, and his irrigation scheme.[3] By 1859, he had a plan drawn up for the canals by surveyor Ebenezer Hadley and acquired the endorsement of U.S. geologist William P. Blake. Blake, having recently conducted a rail survey through the Mojave Desert, concluded that with proper irrigation from the Colorado, a "greater portion of the desert could be made to yield crops of almost any kind."[4] Wozencraft employed this endorsement to convince the California State Assembly to grant him title to 6,635,520 acres of land in the Salton Sink area. The land grant stipulated that Wozencraft, in return, must provide a stable supply of fresh water along the route from San Gorgona Pass to Fort Yuma. Final acquisition of the land titles, however, required U.S. congressional approval.[5]

Gaining federal approval for the massive land grant turned out to be an insurmountable task for the doctor. Though he came close to gaining passage of such bills in 1863 and 1875, his efforts repeatedly met with failure.[6] Finally, his numerous trips to Washington and extensive lobbying efforts on behalf of the land grant and irrigation project came to an abrupt end in a Washington, D.C., boarding house in November 1887. A few days after congressmen derided his latest attempt to gain approval of his irrigation bill as "an old man's folly," Wozencraft unexpectedly passed away.[7] Yet "folly" or not, the idea of diverting Colorado River waters into the desert lived on.

Within five years of the doctor's death, a new and more successful proponent arrived. This man, Charles Robinson Rockwood, formed the California Development Company (CDC) for the purpose of irrigating the desert lands in the vicinity of the Salton Sink. Rockwood proposed that a main canal cut into the west bank of the Colorado and controlled by mechanical headgates could deliver water via gravity feed to a series of irrigation ditches in the Colorado Desert. He predicted that after settlers rushed in to claim the newly irrigated land the CDC would earn a sizable profit by selling the water that flowed through their canal to the newly established farmers.[8]

After some difficulty finding investors to supply the estimated $150,000 construction costs, Rockwood's plan caught the attention of well-known California engineer George Caffey. Caffey realized the profit potential of irrigated desert. He offered to raise the funds and serve as chief engineer in exchange for majority interest in the company for five years. Now facing the prospect of bankruptcy before the project could even get off of the ground, Rockwood and his associates at the CDC accepted Caffey's terms.[9]

The CDC, with Caffey at the helm, promptly began construction on the canals, along with an advertising campaign to lure prospective settlers. Highlighting the Homestead and Desert Land acts (1862, 1877), company brochures promised settlers an agricultural paradise for $1.25 an acre in tracts of up to 320 acres. Further, at Caffey's behest, the campaign marketed the Colorado Desert lands under a more fitting name: the Imperial Valley.[10] Even the *New York Times* got caught up in the euphoria around this attempt to conquer the desert for profitable bounty. The paper reported on April 25, 1901, that the "progress of civilization" had allowed humanity the ability to "redeem" and "make wonderfully fertile" some 1,500 square miles of land in California's Colorado Desert. With this diversion of Colorado River waters and the subsequent blooming of the desert, readers were told to expect "great climatic changes" in what, until this point, had been an "arid waste."[11]

Such boosterism paid off. As early as 1900, homesteaders began arriving in the Imperial Valley. Quickly, new settlements appeared at Calexico, Brawley, Imperial, and Blue Lake. By May 14, 1901, when the main headgate was opened and water began flowing down the canal to "reclaimed" desert farmland, over 1,500 farmers had already settled on the land. By 1904, their land had greened and the presence of 10,000 farmers residing in the Imperial Valley suggested that Wozencraft's idea had been anything but "folly."[12]

Unfortunately for all involved, Wozencraft and Rockford had both ignored a warning that accompanied U.S. geologist William Blake's 1859 "endorsement" of the feasibility of irrigating areas of the Mojave with Colorado River water. Specifically, Blake cautioned that the topography of the area could facilitate the river abandoning its channel once its bank was breached. The river then would permanently empty into the Salton Sink. In this worst-case scenario, it might easily become impossible to return the river to its traditional channel. As a result, large sections of interior and southern California would be submerged under a vast inland sea.[13]

In the spring of 1904, events converged to make the worst-case scenario a reality. Recent floods had deposited a heavy layer of silt that blocked the canal's intake. Rockwood, having recently bought up enough stock to regain control of the CDC from Caffey and facing lawsuits from settlers to whom he had promised water, chose reckless action over bankruptcy. Without adequate study or preparation, he ordered workers to bypass the blocked intake by cutting a new one into the Colorado's bank farther downstream in Mexico. Pressed for time, he also bypassed the safety measure of constructing a headgate at the mouth of the new canal. Rockford assumed this could be dealt with later, after the return of water soothed the angry farmers.[14] Time, though, was not on his side.

In early March 1905, another major flood engorged the Colorado River. The whirling waters cut into its bank at the new intake point, opening a 60-foot-wide breach. Although quickly dammed with brush and sandbags, a second flood on March 18 reopened and enlarged the breach to 90 feet. This time the gap could not be closed, and river water rushed uncontrolled into the Imperial Valley. In November, yet another flood hit, and the water in the Salton Sink had obtained a depth of 60 feet and an area of 150 square miles.[15] Just as Blake warned, the river had abandoned its course in favor of gravity and was in the process of submerging a significant portion of southern California.

In attempting to plug the ill-designed Mexican intake canal, Rockwood quickly depleted what little capital the CDC had acquired. Desperate, he then turned over control of the company to Edward H. Harriman's Southern Pacific Railway in exchange for a $200,000 "loan." For the time being, the Southern Pacific retained the service of Rockwood as chief engineer. Harriman, sensing an opportunity to profit from Imperial Valley produce shipments, had reason to help the irrigation project succeed. Furthermore, as waters in the Salton Sink rose, they threatened to wash away Southern Pacific railways. Eventually, this fear was warranted, as the company lost some 60 miles of track to flood waters.[16]

As Rockwood proved unable to stem the flow of the Colorado River into the Salton Sink, the Southern Pacific replaced him with their own Henry T. Cory as chief engineer. Simultaneously, Harriman came under pressure from the highest levels of government to plug the gap and stop the flooding immediately. Dire forecasts of doom spurred the government to action, as experts predicted the complete inundation of southern California and parts of Arizona. Further, a substantial waterfall had formed in the desert and was cutting back toward the Mexican intake at an alarming rate. If allowed to reach the river channel, experts concluded that it would be impossible to return the river to its traditional path. Fearing such a consequence, President

Theodore Roosevelt publicly urged Harriman to commit all resources at his disposal.[17]

Finally, on February 10, 1907, Southern Pacific engineers succeeded in turning the river. The effort had taken an army of workers seven attempts at building a dam, and every company freight train in the Southwest to haul materials. The cost to the Southern Pacific was in the millions and the damage to local farming catastrophic. What had been the Salton Sink was transformed into the Salton Sea, a 72-feet-deep inland body of water sprawled across 300,000 acres.[18]

The saga of the Imperial Canal and the Salton Sea reveals one influence supporting the reclamation mindset, the dangers of reckless attempts to alter nature, and an increasing perception of a need to control the wild Colorado. If the region was to develop and prosper, the Colorado had to be harnessed and attempts to distribute its water well regulated. The Salton Sea ecological and economic disaster highlighted the inability of private enterprise to accomplish such a grand endeavor. Far from silencing demands for effective and efficient agricultural irrigation, this failure prompted the government to take a more active role in assuring large-scale water delivery. In turn, this enabled development of the nation's arid Southwest well beyond agriculture. The shift of reclamation control from the private sector to government hands paved the way for the eventual construction of Boulder (Hoover) Dam, domination of the Colorado River, and the urbanized American Southwest as we know it today.[19] It also enabled increased water-based recreational opportunities for a growing southwestern population.

The U.S. government had set the stage for this more active role in dominating the West's free-flowing waters when President Theodore Roosevelt signed the Reclamation Act in June 1902. The act, which was the final product of a long and hotly contested debate over the federal role in reclaiming arid lands dating back to at least the 1850s, placed far-reaching powers over western waters in the hands of the Department of Interior. In fact, it promised to initiate what at the time would be the largest public works program in the nation's history.[20] Specifically, it created a "reclamation fund" from the sale of public lands in western states to be used for the construction of irrigation works, authorized the Secretary of the Interior to order and direct investigations into suitable sites for reservoirs and the development of irrigation systems, and gave the secretary the power to withdraw from the public domain any lands required for such enterprises.[21]

Within five years, as the Salton Sea saga unfolded, the Reclamation Service—established in 1902 with the Reclamation Act, separated from the U.S. Geological Survey in 1907, then placed under Interior's control and renamed the U.S. Bureau of Reclamation (USBR)—had selected some twenty-eight reclamation projects throughout the West. These projects ranged from irrigating as few as 8,000 acres in Kansas to 200,000 in Arizona. Most focused on land irrigation for agricultural development, much of which was initiated in former desert lands.[22]

California's Imperial Valley offered the perfect setting for one such project. Beginning in the early twentieth century and marked by extraordinary failures, efforts to irrigate the desert valley with Colorado River water had drawn in thousands of families by the late 1910s. By this time, private projects had, despite inadvertently creating the Salton Sea, managed to make the desert green, profitable, and supportive of a growing population. Yet locals experienced ongoing problems with the silting of canals, fluctuating water levels, and, increasingly, interference by the Mexican government concerning portions of the irrigation canals running through Mexican territory. Subsequently, support grew for the construction of a canal to traverse only American territory. By 1917 the Imperial Irrigation District (IID) began a push for the construction of such a canal. The IID's attorney, Phil Swing, launched a lobbying campaign to acquire congressional approval for the project. Swing succeeded both in getting himself elected to Congress to represent the district and having an All-American Canal Bill placed before Congress. He then looked on in dismay as the bill suffered defeat, primarily as a result of the opposition efforts of Reclamation Service Director Arthur Powell Davis.[23]

Davis's opposition to the All-American Canal Bill had nothing to do with a disagreement over the need for—or the beneficial nature of—the proposed canal. Instead, his concern centered on the idea of the canal as a private enterprise. Having already witnessed the earlier Imperial Canal fiasco, he believed that only government could adequately oversee projects of such magnitude. Further, Davis already had a far grander plan in mind for the Colorado River that included exactly such a canal. This plan, the genesis of which took place during his years in the Colorado River Basin working as a Reclamation Service engineer, called for no less than development of the river's entire drainage area through a series of large-scale reservoirs.

Congress, in agreement with Davis's contention that such projects were beyond the capability of private industry, approved Davis's alternative plan and ordered a comprehensive study of the development of the river basin.[24]

This study resulted in the Fall-Davis Report. Released in 1922, the report called for the construction of a dam "at or near Boulder Canyon" on the Nevada and Arizona state line, to be financed by government funds. The prohibitive cost of construction was to be paid by the sale of electricity to cities in southern California. Further, after completion of the dam brought the river's cyclical flooding under control, the government would finance the construction of the All-American Canal to stabilize irrigation in the Imperial Valley.[25]

As momentum grew for controlling and utilizing Colorado River waters, the USBR set out to find the most suitable location for the river's first reservoir. Investigators took into consideration three primary characteristics in preparing a short list of potential dam sites: geological and topographical features, storage capacity of a potential reservoir, and proximity to existing transportation. Preliminary examinations in April 1920 indicated that Boulder Canyon was the best site, based on its granite bedrock. Black Canyon was named as a second but less-desirable choice because of its weaker volcanic bedrock. Both sites offered reservoir possibilities with adequate storage capacity, were within about 30 miles of the Union Pacific Railroad, and were within reasonable distance to southern California for the economical distribution of electricity.[26]

This preliminary nod to the Boulder Canyon site served as the basis for the Fall-Davis Report's use of the term "at or near Boulder Canyon" as its recommended dam site, but a final decision had not been reached at the time of the report's release. This enabled Phil Swing to attach the name Boulder Canyon to the first congressional bill introduced for the project. The name stuck. Popular media embraced it, and it appeared on subsequent bills, including the successful Boulder Canyon Project Act of 1928.[27]

Between January 1921 and April 1923, a team of fifty-eight Reclamation Service investigators led by engineer Walker Young conducted a careful examination of both the Boulder Canyon and Black Canyon sites. They established a camp at the first gravel beach, approximately one-quarter to one-half mile upstream of the mouth of Boulder Canyon.[28] Utilizing flat-bottom oar boats and outboard-propelled boats to examine three possible sites in the canyon, the group was not impressed with the Boulder Canyon options. They eventually decided that only one location within the canyon could possibly support a dam over 500 feet tall.[29]

Testing the sites' suitability had not been an easy process. It required extensive and dangerous core drilling in the riverbed and adjoining canyon walls to determine geological suitability. This presented a problem, as mid-river drilling had to be conducted from floating platforms that obviously lacked adequate stability. Young solved this problem by devising a system that anchored the drilling platforms to canyon walls. Heavy ringbolts were secured in the cliff faces and then used as anchors attached to large steel support cables. The support cables were then attached to the drilling barges and stretched tightly. Although this system provided stability for drilling, it did nothing to protect the drillers against the Colorado's legendary floods. Such floods presented a constant danger, as workers frequently found themselves swept from the barges and into the angry water with little or no warning. Surprisingly, most were retrieved, with only one man losing his life in this manner.[30]

After their disappointing investigation of Boulder Canyon, the group moved downstream to a beach camp just below Black Canyon. There, they continued to face dangers from floods and the strong winds that funneled southward through the canyon. On one occasion, shortly after setting up camp, a gale completely destroyed their camp, ripping up wooden planking and decimating supplies. Undeterred, the group commenced drilling in the winter of 1922. After quickly determining an initial site to be unsuitable, they moved to a secondary choice, which they labeled Site D. After months of drilling and sampling bedrock, they sent final core samples and data to Denver for analysis in the spring of 1923.[31]

Much to everyone's relief, the USBR analysts determined that the Black Canyon site was suitable for the dam's construction. A primary rationale for the choice was that geologists discovered unacceptable jointing and faulting of the granite bedrock beneath Boulder Canyon. Further, the Black Canyon site was superior to any place found within Boulder Canyon in several additional regards: it required less removal of gravel and silt; canyon wall geology allowed for easier tunneling; the gorge was narrower and thus easier to dam; it would create a larger capacity reservoir; and nearby sand beds could be mined for mixing concrete. A final consideration was easier access to the Black Canyon site by way of Las Vegas, as opposed to Boulder Canyon

FIGURE 2.1. The Black Canyon of the Colorado River prior to construction of Boulder Dam, 1920s. Courtesy of University of Nevada Las Vegas Libraries Special Collections.

by way of St. Thomas.[32] Walker Young later recalled the relief of engineers when he reported that a standard gauge railway could easily be constructed from the Las Vegas vicinity to the Black Canyon site.[33] Although known as the Boulder Canyon Project, the dam would be built in Black Canyon.

As site selection was nearing completion in 1923, and the majority of affected states had approved the Colorado River Compact, it seemed as though Congress would likely pass an enabling act for the project sooner rather than later. Once informed of the states' agreement, Congressman Phil Swing and Senator Hiram Johnson of California introduced the Boulder Canyon Project Bill in 1923. Congress, however, refused to approve the bill until the three-year site selection study was formally completed. Then, Arizona further muddied the process through its energetic opposition to the Colorado River Compact. Arizona congressmen and attorneys stalled the bill's approval via numerous filibusters and legal maneuvers. The Boulder Canyon Project Act would not pass both houses of Congress and be signed into law until December 19, 1928.[34]

The Boulder Canyon Project Act opened the long-blocked path for construction of the first reservoir on the Colorado River. The act stipulated that the purpose of the reservoir would be to store water for the reclamation of public lands, to generate electricity, control floods, improve navigation, and regulate the flow of the river. It further provided that a canal would be built to the Imperial Valley located wholly within the United States. In regard to financing, the act created the Colorado River Dam Fund under control of the Secretary of the Treasury. The budget for the massive undertaking was set at $165 million, to be repaid through the sale of generated electricity.[35] Recently seated President Herbert Hoover declared the act effective on June 25, 1929, despite the continued refusal of Arizona to ratify the Compact.[36]

Regardless of lingering opposition, the project raced ahead. The dam's construction officially began on September 17, 1930, as Secretary of the Interior Ray Lyman Wilbur ceremoniously drove the first spike in the Union Pacific's spur line to the site. The clang of Secretary Wilbur's hammer set in motion a massive program of construction. By the time of its completion a mere five years later, the Colorado River would be blocked by the world's largest dam, which impounded the world's largest man-made reservoir.[37] The West would have a new major source of electricity, irrigation water, and, of course, water-based recreational opportunities.

When completed, the dam stood 727 feet tall, 650 feet wide at base, 45 feet wide at top, and had a crest length of 1,180 feet. In all, the dam structure weighed an estimated 6,500,000 tons and contained some 4,000,000 cubic yards of concrete—enough to pave a 20-foot-wide road from California to Florida. Yet those numbers reveal only part of the monumental task. When one also considers site preparation and logistical requirements, the accomplishment becomes even more awe-inspiring. Some 9,000,000 tons of rock and over 1,000,000 tons of river sediment had to be removed before construction could even begin. Further, an incomprehensible amount of supplies had to be delivered to the site. These included 5,000,000 barrels of cement, 165,000 train carloads of sand, 35,000 tons of reinforcement steel, 900 train carloads of hydraulic machinery, and more than 1,000 miles of steel pipe. The total amount of supplies, if placed in one train, would stretch from Boulder City, Nevada, to Kansas City, Missouri.[38]

On top of the dam, Norwegian-born sculptor Oskar J. W. Hansen designed a monument to honor what he perceived as the exceptional American spirit and character that allowed for such a monumental undertaking. To him, the structure represented a wonder on par with the Great Pyramids, the Acropolis, and the Roman Colosseum. Just as each of those magnificent structures symbolized the genius of each civilization, so did the dam portray America's power, skill, and ingenuity. Echoing Frederick Jackson Turner's "Frontier Thesis," Hansen characterized the building of the dam as a pinnacle act of daring carried out by a "virile type of man" shaped by "the settling of this continent" and "inured through constant adjustments into quickness of wit." His monument, which he aptly named Winged Figures of the Republic, consists of two 30-foot-tall bronze statues that reflect what he saw as the American-type of physiognomy. This facial shape and expression had been "beaten by privations and the strong winds of mountain and plain" to resemble "the look of eagles."[39]

Cast of three-quarter-inch-thick bronze, the two identical seated figures with wings upstretched guard a 142-foot tall flagpole. The flagpole erupts from a base of polished black diorite chosen by the artist for its luster. Embedded within the diorite floor, one sees the great seal of the United States, the signs of the zodiac, and a large astronomical map and universal clock that pinpoints the exact date and time of the dam's dedication. Further commenting on American power and the historical significance of the dam, the monument's star map lists such important historical events as the birth of Christ and the completion of the pyramids. The date immortalized on Hansen's universal clock is September 30, 1935.[40]

While such comparisons may be overblown, the dam and its reservoir were monumentally impressive. When filled to capacity, the reservoir reached from the dam at the mouth of Black Canyon, north to within a few miles of Overton, Nevada, then east past Pearce Ferry to the gate of the Grand Canyon itself. It was 115 miles long, 582 feet deep, and claimed a shoreline of 550 miles. Its glimmering surface area measured 227 square miles. In all, its 30.5-million-acre-feet capacity would account for enough water to submerge the entire state of Connecticut ten feet deep.[41]

Naturally, the filling of such a large reservoir attracted significant public attention, sustained by frequent reports in local and national media outlets chronicling the lake's level and reiterating the point that it would be the world's largest reservoir. Through such reports, locals could track the lake's progress as it grew in length to seventy-three miles, eighty-four miles, and so on. Other reports listed the daily fill rate, measuring rises in water levels to one-tenth of a foot. Finally, project engineer Walker Young informed the

FIGURE 2.2. One of Oskar Hansen's Winged Figures of the Republic atop Boulder Dam, 1930s. Courtesy of the United States Bureau of Reclamation.

FIGURE 2.3. Fishing in the reservoir from a National Park Service boat, 1939. Courtesy of National Park Service Historic Photograph Collection, photographer George A. Grant.

public that, on July 5, 1935, "Boulder Lake" had officially claimed the title of world's largest man-made reservoir. That day, in reaching a capacity of 4,100,000 acre-feet, the lake surpassed the previous record set by Egypt's Aswan Old Dam, completed in 1902.[42]

Such articles also shaped the public's expectations regarding additional uses by including accounts of how the ever-growing body of water offered new recreational opportunities of "considerable value." Early reports commented on how fun-seekers could already enjoy boating, fishing, swimming, and waterskiing by mid-1935. Charter boats also stood ready for sightseeing trips throughout the reaches of the lake and to the upper face of the dam. Those wishing to swim in the new lake could do so with a relative sense of safety, as the Bureau of Reclamation had placed lifeguards on duty as early as 1935.[43]

People from across the nation took note of the recreational opportunities afforded by the new lake, along with a significant degree of curiosity concerning the dam and its construction. Such interest was evident as early as 1934, as visitors flocked to Boulder City to have a look at the dam site and the earliest stages of the lake. In February of that year, the very month that water began to fill the reservoir, tourists had already overwhelmed Boulder City's capacity. On the weekend of February 10–11, over 3,500 people arrived. With the town's only two hotels—Boulder Dam Hotel and Boulder City Auto Court—completely filled, city officials turned to creative solutions for housing visitors. In one such measure, they transformed the local jail into a makeshift hotel. At least twenty tourists gained the added experience of sleeping in jail cells. Many others found shelter in nearby Las Vegas, either in hotels or, surprisingly often, in the houses of willing residents.[44]

Visitation continued to increase in the years immediately following. The opening of Highway 93 across the top of the dam added to this trend by rendering the structure and its surrounding area more accessible to automobiles. This road became a very popular transportation artery, as it provided a connection between U.S. Route 66 at Kingman, Arizona; the dam; Boulder City; and Las Vegas. Even with strict limitations in effect, over 7,500 people traversed the dam via the roadway during its first ten weeks of use in early 1936. An additional 30,000 made the journey from Kingman to view the dam during the same period.[45]

This influx of visitors did not catch the USBR or government entirely by surprise. The USBR had noticed as far back as the 1910s that dam projects tended to draw large numbers of recreationists. By the time of the Boulder Dam project, bureau director Elwood Mead was convinced the reservoir was destined to be a "tourist Mecca."[46] Further, actions of individuals associated with the bureau, the NPS, and other departments of government indicate a strong concern for how recreational activity would be managed at the world's largest reservoir.

As the USBR's expertise centered on managing water rather than recreation, the NPS seemed the obvious choice to oversee the areas' recreational aspects. There was, however, the significant problem of the two agencies' historical friction and conflicting mandates. With USBR intent on the domination and transformation of the natural landscape, and the NPS working for the preservation and enjoyment of the same landscape, there seemed little if any room for cooperation. The early twentieth-century controversy over the damming of Yosemite's Hetch Hetchy Valley had, in effect, birthed the NPS. But in this instance there was room for compromise, as both the USBR and NPS stood to benefit from some sort of cooperative arrangement. The USBR could shed itself of the unwanted responsibility of recreational management, and the NPS could expand its holdings and role in recreational management, even if only reluctantly by some. The Department of Interior certainly recognized the benefits of such an arrangement to all involved, as in 1929 Secretary Wilbur instructed both the USBR and NPS to consult with one another to figure out how to work out the future joint management of the site.[47]

With the need for an established arrangement and the Department of Interior pushing interagency cooperation, the problem was now for the NPS to assume a management role over recreational activities without compromising its preservation mandate. In 1929, Secretary Wilbur supported the idea of designating the area between Zion National Park and the Colorado River as the Virgin National Park. The NPS balked at the suggestion because the area failed to meet its national park criteria. Among other problems, it was found to lack the necessary scenic quality, was centered on a man-made object, and was heavily utilized by ranching and mining interests.[48]

Following the failure to establish an area-wide national park, Wilbur maintained that at least a portion must be removed from the public domain and in some way managed by the NPS. At his insistence, President Herbert Hoover withdrew 4,212 square miles from the public domain in April 1930. Two years later, Wilbur assigned special assistant and former Michigan congressman Louis Cramton to investigate how the NPS could assume control of recreational activities in the area. Cramton's study concluded that the withdrawn land should be divided into two sections. The eastern section should be designated part of the Grand Canyon National Monument; the western section, including the dam and its reservoir, should be part of a new type of NPS unit. Characterizing this innovative unit as a "recreational reservation," Cramton called for the establishment of the Boulder Canyon National Reservation.[49]

Congress did not seem to share Interior's enthusiasm for this new NPS unit. A bill to create the reservation, primarily drafted by the department, was introduced in 1933 by Nevada and Arizona congressmen. Although largely unopposed by conservation groups, the bill failed to pass. Instead, it failed because Nevada's own Senator Tasker Oddie believed that the U.S. government had overstepped its constitutional limits and violated Nevada sovereignty in its development and administration of Boulder City. He was subsequently unwilling to allow further federal control in the area.[50]

Meanwhile, the number of visitors to the dam area continued to grow. In 1935, the Boulder Dam Reservation bill was reintroduced in Congress, only to become stalled once more. As the situation called for immediate action, the USBR and NPS began negotiating between themselves to divide administrative duties there. On October 16, 1936, the negotiations bore fruit, when the two agencies issued a Memorandum of Agreement for joint management of the area that had been removed from the public domain for the purposes of the construction of Boulder Dam and the impoundment of its reservoir. It stated that such an agreement was necessary, given congressional inaction, and "a large number of visitors used the lands and waters of the Boulder Canyon Project Area for purposes of recreation." It further stated that "the National Park Service has the authority and funds for the administration, protection and maintenance of the recreational activities."[51]

The agreement specifically provided that the USBR would retain jurisdiction, authority, and responsibility for Boulder Dam, appurtenant works, Boulder City, and lands immediately adjacent to the dam. The NPS received jurisdiction over all other areas within the reservation boundaries. Water flow, storage, and utilization remained under the USBR, and the "accomplishment" of such purposes was to remain the "dominant consideration" in the administration of the area. The USBR retained the authority to settle any controversies that developed as a result of the dual focus on reclamation and recreation. In regard to leases that might affect concessionaires at Boulder Dam or Boulder City, the NPS was to gain approval from the USBR. In turn, the USBR was also required to seek NPS approval for the granting of concession leases at Boulder Dam or Boulder City that might affect existing concessionaires in other parts of the area. If agreement proved elusive regarding concessions, the Secretary of the Interior held the deciding vote. All income received from NPS concession leases, licenses, and permits was to go to the Colorado River Dam Fund.[52]

In addition to defining territorial control and outlining the division of powers, the agreement laid out the specific functions granted to each entity. The NPS was charged with the development of the area, including roads, trails, and other facilities. It was granted the power of establishing and granting contracts for such development, as well as for recreational purposes. These included boating, hiking, camping, swimming, and sightseeing. No individual contracts could exceed twenty years in length, but could be renewed. The NPS also received the power to grant contracts for the operation of the Boulder City Airport.

In regard to behavior and safety within the area, the agreement granted the NPS authority to set all rules and regulations for the recreational areas. Further, it was to maintain rangers, educators, lifeguards, and other services to ensure safety and full usage of the area. The NPS could set and enforce regulations regarding the conservation of historical or archaeological remains and oversee all investigation and excavation of such sites. At its discretion, the NPS could establish museums for the display of such items.

The NPS also could set and enforce policies related to the occupation or leasing of lands within the area for purposes unrelated to the construction or work on the dam, Boulder City, or the reservoir. Specifically, mining and grazing would be allowed to continue under NPS supervision within area boundaries. The NPS agreed to control transportation in the area in regard to land, water, and air, with the exception of transportation required for the USBR to carry out its functions. NPS authority also extended to the conservation and protection of area wildlife, which was to be coordinated with the Bureau of Biological Survey. Finally, the NPS was to provide advice and recommendations to the USBR regarding resort and recreational developments within Boulder City.[53]

The agreement also listed the specific functions of the USBR in regard to the administration of the lands and structures placed under its jurisdiction. First, as mentioned, it was to oversee the operation of the dam, reservoir, and related engineering works, and retain control over Boulder City. Its authority over Boulder City included governmental administration, law enforcement, recreational development, and the granting of leases, permits, and licenses. Regarding recreational development decisions relative to Boulder City, or that might affect recreational developments in NPS-controlled areas, the USBR was to consult with the NPS. The bureau also agreed to supply a facility within Boulder City to accommodate NPS administrators. Concerning public visits to the dam, the USBR received the power to establish rules for such visits and to control traffic on roads and water providing access to the dam and its immediate works. Once tourists arrived at the dam, the USBR was responsible for providing them with guides, lectures, and information to help them understand its history and operation.[54]

The USBR's and NPS's establishment of a recreational area speaks of how the river and the idea of the river had undergone yet another transformation by the 1930s. Water had fully replaced minerals as the area's most valuable resource. Its worth resided not only in irrigation, drinking water, and electricity production, but in recreational capacity as well. Reservoir-based recreation had arrived on a massive scale with NPS blessing.

With the taming of the river, the immediate and only somewhat anticipated wave of recreational demands had threatened to overwhelm the unprepared USBR. The government was forced to react by creating an administered recreation area. In so doing, it recognized the significance of outdoor recreation for its citizenry. Even beyond such recognition and reaction, the government assumed a very difficult regulatory and management responsibility over such activities and opportunities. As reservoir water resources also supplied electricity and irrigation, the NPS entered into an unenviable position in agreeing to manage the new national recreation area. The NPS would subsequently be charged with supplying the recreational needs of a public dependent upon the same water source for its enjoyment, sustainability, and growth. In the ensuing decades, this would be no easy task, as public belief in free and unlimited use of the reservoir and surrounding landscape grew alongside increased demands for water, safety, and preservation of the environment.

NOTES

1. Foster Rhea Dulles, *A History of Recreation: America Learns to Play* (New York: Appleton-Century Crofts, 1965), vii.

2. Joseph E. Stevens, *Hoover Dam: An American Adventure* (Norman: University of Oklahoma Press, 1988), 8–9.

3. "Dr. O. M. Wozencraft; Cortes," *Daily Democratic State Journal,* 28 June 1855; "Legal Intelligence," *San Francisco Daily Evening Bulletin,* 13 December 1856; "Organization of the Pacific Railroad Convention," *San Francisco Daily Bulletin,* 21 September 1859.

4. Stevens, *Hoover Dam,* 9.

5. "The Wozencraft Project in San Diego County," *San Francisco Bulletin,* 3 December 1859; "Letter from Sacramento," *San Francisco Bulletin,* 26 February 1863.

6. "Letter from Sacramento," *San Francisco Bulletin,* 26 February 1863; "From the National Capital," *Daily Evening Bulletin,* 19 December 1876; "Washington," *Arizona Weekly Miner,* 23 February 1877; "Washington Telegraphic Items," *Daily Evening Bulletin,* 4 April 1878; Donald Worster, *Rivers of Empire: Water, Aridity, and the Growth of the American West* (New York: Oxford University Press, 1992), 195–96.

7. "Death of Dr. Wozencraft," *Daily Evening Bulletin,* 24 November 1887.

8. Stevens, *Hoover Dam,* 11.

9. Ibid.; Steven Greenfield, "A Lake by Mistake," *American Heritage of Invention and Technology Magazine* 21 (winter 2006):38–49; Helen Hosmer, "Imperial Valley: Triumph and Failure in the Colorado Desert," *The American West* 3 (winter 1966):39.

10. Hosmer, "Imperial Valley," 39; Stevens, *Hoover Dam*, 11.

11. "Redeeming the Colorado," *New York Times,* 25 April 1901.

12. Stevens, *Hoover Dam,* 11–12; Worster, *Rivers of Empire,* 196; Greenfield, "A Lake by Mistake"; "Colorado Desert Blooms," *New York Times,* 28 December 1902.

13. Lloyd Woerner, "The Creation of the Salton Sea: An Engineering Folly," *Journal of the West* 28 (January 1989):110; Hosmer, "Imperial Valley," 38.

14. Greenfield, "A Lake by Mistake"; Woerner, "The Creation of the Salton Sea," 110–11; Stevens, *Hoover Dam,* 12–13.

15. Stevens, *Hoover Dam,* 14.

16. Hosmer, "Imperial Valley," 45–46; Woerner, "The Creation of the Salton Sea," 111; Greenfield, "A Lake by Mistake"; "Railroad to Retreat," *New York Times,* 4 July 1906.

17. Greenfield, "A Lake by Mistake"; Stevens, *Hoover Dam,* 15; "Irrigation Making a New Sea," *New York Times,* 24 September 1905; "Demand on Harriman Made By President," *New York Times,* 21 December 1906; "Quick Work by Harriman: Trains Rushed to Colorado River Break After President's Demand," *New York Times,* 22 December 1906.

18. "The Colorado Controlled," *New York Times,* 12 February 1907; "The Colorado Restrained," *New York Times,* 31 July 1907; Greenfield, "A Lake by Mistake"; Stevens, *Hoover Dam,* 15; Woerner, "The Creation of the Salton Sea," 112; Hosmer, "Imperial Valley," 47.

19. Marc Resiner, *Cadillac Desert: The American West and Its Disappearing Water,* revised edition (New York: Penguin, 1993), 3. Resisner points out that, in reality, reclamation succeeded in greening only a section of the West comparable in size to the state of Missouri. However, its influence regarding unsustainable urban growth, agriculture, and attitudes in a marginal land were tremendous.

20. Donald J. Pisani, *To Reclaim a Divided West: Water, Law, and Public Policy, 1848–1902* (Albuquerque: University of New Mexico Press, 1992), 274–75; Donald J. Pisani, "Federal Reclamation and the American West," *Agricultural History* 77 (summer 2003):393.

21. *Reclamation Act of 1902* (U.S. Public, No. 161).

22. Pisani, "Federal Reclamation and the American West," 394; Bureau of Reclamation, "The Bureau of Reclamation: A Very Brief History," http://www.usbr.gov/history /borhist.html (accessed February 23, 2016).

23. Stevens, *Hoover Dam,* 15–17.

24. Ibid., 17.

25. Ibid., 17–18; United States Senate, "Problems of Imperial Valley and Vicinity," (U.S. Senate Document 142, 67th Congress, February 23, 1922), 21.

26. Stevens, Hoover Dam, 19.

27. Ibid., 26.

28. Edna Jackson Ferguson, interview reproduced in Andrew J. Dunbar and Dennis McBride, *Building Hoover Dam: An Oral History of the Great Depression* (New York: Twayne Publishers, 1993), 2–6.

29. Stevens, *Hoover Dam,* 20–21; Walker Young, interview reproduced in Dunbar and McBride, *Building Hoover Dam,* 1–2, 6.

30. Stevens, *Hoover Dam,* 21–22.

31. Ibid., 24.

32. Ibid., 24–25.

33. Young, interview in Dunbar and McBride, *Building Hoover Dam,* 6.

34. For in-depth discussion of the Colorado River Compact, see Norris Hundley Jr., *Water in the West: The Colorado River Compact and the Politics of Water in the American West* (Berkeley: University of California Press, 1975), passim; Linda J. Lear, "Boulder Dam: A Crossroads in Natural Resource Policy," *Journal of the West* 24 (October 1985):84–85; "Boulder Dam Bill Passes the Senate," *New York Times,* 15 December 1928; "Boulder Dam Bill Sent to Coolidge," *New York Times,* 19 December 1928; "President Signs Boulder Dam Bill," *New York Times,* 22 December 1928.

35. *Boulder Canyon Project Act,* Pub. L. No. 70–642, 45 Stat. 1057 (1928).

36. Herbert Hoover, Proclamation No. 1882 (June 25, 1929).

37. Walker R. Young, "Hoover Dam: Purpose, Plans, and Progress of Construction," *Scientific American* 147 (September 1932):135.

38. Committee Appointed by the Associated General Contractors of America and the American Engineering Council, "Report on Hoover Dam Project and Present Status" (December 1931), 3–4 (hereafter: Contractors and Engineering Council, "Report on Hoover Dam Project").

39. Hansen, Oskar J. W., "With the Look of Eagles," in *The Sculptures at Boulder Dam,* Pamphlet, Washington, D.C., Bureau of Reclamation, United States Department of Interior (May 1942), 1–4. UNLV Special Collections, Call# NB237 H25 A49 1942.

40. Ibid.; Hansen, Oskar J. W., "A Split Second Petrified on the Face of the Universal Clock," in *The Sculptures at Boulder Dam,* Pamphlet, U.S. Dept. of the Interior.

41. Contractors and Engineering Council, "Report on Hoover Dam Project," 39; E. H. Heinemann, "Colorado River History Told by Government Officer," *Las Vegas Evening Review-Journal,* 22 April 1936.

42. "Boulder Lake 84 Miles Long," *Las Vegas Evening Review-Journal,* 29 July 1935; "Boulder Lake Holding Its Own," *Las Vegas Evening Review-Journal,* 31 July 1935; "Man Made Dimple," *Literary Digest,* 3 August 1935, 17; Walker Young, "Boulder Lake Is Now Largest Man-Made Reservoir in the World," *Las Vegas Evening Review-Journal,* 24 August 1935; "Lake Mead, Largest Man-Made," *Scientific American* 158 (February 1938):108–09.

43. Young, "Boulder Lake is Now Largest," *Las Vegas Evening Review-Journal,* 24 August 1935.

44. "Dam Destined to Grow as Tourist Hub," *Las Vegas Evening Review-Journal,* 10 January 1934; "All Tourist Records Fall On Week End," *Las Vegas Evening Review-Journal,* 12 February 1934.

45. "Tourist Travel to Dam is Increasing," *Las Vegas Evening Review-Journal,* 3 March 1934; "Tourist Records Broken for Dam," *Las Vegas Evening Review-Journal,* 6 March 1934; "Road Over Boulder Dam Open Tomorrow," *Las Vegas Evening Review-Journal,* 11 December 1935; "They've Streamed in Via Kingman to Cross Dam," *Boulder*

Dam Challenge, 6 March 1936. Early regulations limited automobile passage across the dam to escorted trips every half hour.

46. Elwood Mead quoted in Douglas Dodd, "Boulder Dam Recreation Area: The Bureau of Reclamation, the National Park Service, and the Origins of the National Recreation Area Concept at Lake Mead, 1929–1936," in *The Bureau of Reclamation: History Essays from the Centennial Symposium,* edited by Brit Allan Storey. Denver: U.S. Bureau of Reclamation, 2008, 468. See also, Douglas W. Dodd, "Boulder Dam Recreation Area: The Bureau of Reclamation, The National Park Service, and the Origins of the National Recreation Area Concept at Lake Mead, 1929–1936," *Southern California Quarterly* 88 (winter 2006–2007):431–73.

47. Ibid., 488.

48. Ibid., 476–77.

49. Ibid.

50. Ibid., 477–79.

51. "Memorandum of Agreement Between the National Park Service and the Bureau of Reclamation. Relating to the Development and Administration of the Boulder Canyon Project Area," 29 August 1936, 1. Lake Mead National Recreation Area Folder, Boulder City/Hoover Dam Museum, Boulder City, Nevada. (Hereafter, "Memorandum of Agreement," 29 August 1936).

52. "Memorandum of Agreement," 29 August 1936, 2–3.

53. Ibid., 3–5.

54. Ibid., 5–6.

CHAPTER THREE

Defining a National Recreation Area, 1936–1966

With the completion of Boulder Dam, the federal government also created a world-class tourist attraction. This section of the Colorado River area thus emerged as a popular, federally regulated, outdoor recreational destination overseen by the National Park Service (NPS). In agreeing to the role, the NPS sanctioned both its existence and the idea of large-scale reservoir-based recreation in arid lands. It also accepted a position of power in the modern hydraulic society and the accompanying responsibilities. The thirty-year period from 1936 to 1966 subsequently witnessed the area redefined in terms of free recreational activity and open access. All agencies involved proved very successful at managing the area during this period, so much so that the government ultimately defined national recreation systems based largely on the Lake Mead example. Many of the NRAs, like Lake Mead National Recreation Area (LMNRA), would be managed by the NPS and built around reservoirs that supplied water for both growth and recreation. Simply stated, the concept of the NPS-managed national recreation, birthed in 1936, matured during this period.

By the time the NPS agreed to assume management of the recreation area in 1936, it had already been heavily involved in the development of recreational infrastructure on and around the reservoir. This involvement had taken the form of Civilian Conservation Corps (CCC) work on NPS projects aimed at developing recreational amenities. The NPS projects were completed by two companies of CCC enrollees stationed in Boulder City. These companies, whose combined strength varied from approximately 200 to 500 enrollees, remained active in Boulder City and the recreational area from November 10, 1935, until their disbandment on July 23, 1942.[1] During that time, work completed by the young CCC workers greatly enhanced the recreational accessibility and attributes of the area.[2]

One of the CCC's most significant local projects was the construction of Boulder Beach, just north of Boulder City in Hemenway Wash. Construction

FIGURE 3.1. Lakeview Overlook at Lake Mead National Recreation Area, 2010.
Courtesy of Marianne Molland.

on the beach began in December 1935. CCC workers cleared the area of
rocks, driftwood, and brush and then leveled it. At that point, they distributed truckloads of sand from the high watermark to the current waterline.
They also deposited a large stockpile of sand to be used for beach repair and
extension as required by fluctuations in water level. Between 1936 and 1940,
they built swimming and diving floats, bathhouses and dressing rooms that
could be moved on skids to accommodate changes in water levels, picnic
tables, and benches.[3]

Other CCC projects in the recreation area varied widely. These included
helping with archaeological surveys, highway shouldering, grading run-
ways at the Boulder City Airport, restoring the nine-hole Boulder City Golf
Course, landscaping and concrete work around the National Park Service's
headquarters in Boulder City, clearing the lake's shoreline of debris and
driftwood that endangered boaters, constructing stone walls and wooden
guardrails around parking facilities, installing navigation lights on concrete
columns along the course of the reservoir, conducting surveys of wildlife
species, preliminary work on a proposed "rim of the lake highway," and constructing and operating visitor checkpoints. The latter structures replaced
the original gates to the federal reservation and were located along the highway heading into Boulder City from both the Nevada and Arizona sides.
An additional checkpoint was established on the road leading to Boulder

Beach. CCC workers manned the checkpoints and kept count of individuals entering the area. They did not collect entrance fees, as entrance was free of charge at this time.[4]

The work of the CCC was invaluable to visitors and the NPS for improving access and amenities. The projects enabled the large-scale visitation that was taking place even as the projects were underway. Orientation of the projects set a precedent that the NPS would follow throughout the next three decades. At the recreation area, access and visitor amenities took priority. The period of the late-1930s through the mid-1960s continued to be defined by such action.

In order for any such definition or expansion of access and amenities to occur, the NPS first had to ensure the survival of its prototype recreation area. This required fending off an attempt by Nevada congressman Key Pittman in 1939 to have the federal government remove 8,000 acres of land from the recreation area surrounding the reservoir and placed under state control. Pittman, along with Las Vegas politicians and businessmen, opposed the creation of the national recreation area and the NPS's management role. Specifically, they did not agree with the NPS's power to limit development and oversee concessionaire contracts. Pittman introduced bill transferring the land to the state of Nevada.[5]

Though the bill passed both houses of Congress, its popularity did not extend to the NPS or Interior. Secretary of the Interior Harold Ickes took a particularly strong dislike to the proposal, which he believed was backed by Las Vegas gambling interests. Harold Ickes was certain that these interests wished to establish casinos on the shores of the new reservoir. The secretary disapproved of such activities and detested the idea of having them infiltrate the recreational area. He met with President Roosevelt to stress his opposition to the bill. Subsequently, the president vetoed the bill on August 10, 1939.[6]

In the following decades, public recreational use of Lake Mead increased rapidly. This usage can be attributed to several factors: the expansion of the recreational area's boundaries and the addition of a second large reservoir; contextual influences such as the widespread popularity of automobile tourism and a level of postwar affluence that made vacationing commonplace; and infrastructure improvements to handle growing numbers of recreationists.

Recreational opportunities available at LMNRA increased dramatically in the early 1950s with the completion of a second dam and reservoir some sixty-three miles downstream from Boulder Dam. Efforts to build a dam in this location dated back to 1902 and gained momentum after the construction of Boulder Dam.[7] Following Boulder Dam's completion, the Department of the Interior urged Congress to appropriate funds for a second dam. Congress acted with surprising swiftness and approved the building of Davis Dam in 1941.[8] This dam and its reservoir were to be, in the words of Secretary Ickes, "another great multipurpose" federal project.[9] Once completed, its 1.6 million acre-feet of impounded river water would provide irrigation, electricity, and additional outdoor recreational opportunities.[10] It is telling that, in contrast to the Boulder Dam Project, the government seems to have taken recreational demand into account when defining this dam-building project.

Even though Congress acted swiftly to approve the dam, the onset of World War II delayed its construction by several years. On October 28, 1942, the War Production Board (WPB) ordered an indefinite halt to construction on seven western irrigation projects. Regarding Davis Dam, the WPB order called for the cessation of work on the entire project no later than November 1.[11] Work did not resume on the project until April 22, 1946. When completed in 1951, the dam joined Boulder, Parker, and Imperial dams to create the Colorado River's fourth reservoir. At this point, the U.S. Bureau of Reclamation (USBR) still planned an additional two dams some 150 and 250 miles upriver from Boulder Dam.[12]

With the completion of Davis Dam, the nation's first national recreation area stood geographically complete. Two reservoirs and hundreds of miles of sunbaked water promised trophy fishing, relief from desert heat, and endless variations of water sports. Beyond the shoreline, camping, hiking, and hunting beckoned the mid-century sportsman. This truly seemed a national playground, where the public could exercise what many in the post–World War II period came to view as their right to recreation.

Americans certainly exercised this right with increasing frequency at the recreation area. Water sports emerged as a primary recreational draw early on. Other popular activities included fishing, boating, and waterskiing. In regard to fishing, Las Vegas area hatcheries began stocking the reservoir with bass as soon as waters began rising. The first stocking occurred in 1935

FIGURE 3.2. Boaters on the upper reaches of Lake Mohave, 2010. Photo by author.

and consisted of 14,835 largemouth bass. Local hatcheries released an additional 340,000 bass and 35,000 bluegills during 1937 and 1938. By the early 1940s, the reservoir had already achieved a reputation as a site for exceptional bass fishing.[13]

Media took note of the recreational offerings even before the new reservoir existed. In 1934, for example, the *American Legion Monthly* ran an article predicting the coming reservoir as a fishing destination. It would be so significant, stated author Alexander Gardiner, that it would likely attract large-scale boating and fishing tackle industries to the Las Vegas area. He further reported that Las Vegans were already planning fishing holidays on the future "lake stocked with gamey fish."[14]

Likewise, USBR literature highlighted the value of the reservoir as a fishing and boating destination in the 1930s. The USBR produced a "Construction of Boulder Dam" pamphlet characterizing the reservoir as "a lake being stocked with millions of bass, crappie, and bream." It also drew attention to the trout being stocked in the cooler waters below the dam.[15] Postcards featuring the reservoir also promoted its recreational value as early as 1935. That year, a Boulder Dam postcard book, published by Chicago's Curt Teich and Company, portrayed the lake as a "sportsman's paradise" and "glorious vacation" destination. Some postcard images featured artistic renderings of individuals boating on the lake as well.[16] In 1935, the new dam's place as an American icon was further established by its image on the three-cent postage stamp.[17]

The lake's fame and value as a recreational destination continued to grow throughout the 1940s, '50s, and '60s, abetted by a steady stream of media attention. During the 1940s, articles, advertisements, and pamphlets extolled the lake's boating, fishing, and other recreational opportunities. In 1946, one could find Lake Mead highlighted in *Arizona Highways* as the region's "central attraction" with fishing and boating offering fantastic opportunities for vacationing Americans. The glossy images accompanying the story provided equal incentive for travel in their depictions of Lake Mead revelers enjoying loads of fun in pleasure boats and other water activities under the desert sun.[18]

Tourism industries also helped establish the recreation area as a significant destination in the mid-1940s. Trans World Airlines (TWA), for example, featured Boulder Dam and Lake Mead prominently in advertisements. In a 1946 magazine advertisement, TWA presented the dam and reservoir as American icons of such importance that even seeing them from a plane was a significant occurrence.[19] USBR publications similarly continued to highlight the reservoir as a recreational destination during the 1940s. A pamphlet on Boulder Dam referred to Lake Mead as "a popular boating and bathing resort, as well as a fisherman's paradise."[20]

Such representations continued throughout the 1950s, as the lake became even more known for its boating and trophy fishing. Prospective visitors could find similar pieces gracing the pages of magazines and newspapers with regularity in the decades to follow. A representative 1956 piece, once again in *Arizona Highways,* portrayed the area solely in terms of fishing and boating. In this piece, readers encountered images of boats moored around Emery's Landing in El Dorado Canyon and read of the "fabulous fishing" available on Lake Mead and Lake Mohave. The author went on to refer to Lake Mead as the "Mecca of anglers everywhere."[21] *Nevada Highways,* not to be outdone by its Arizona counterpart, loaded a seven-page feature on the recreation area with real and artistic renderings of pleasure boating, fishing, and waterskiing. Along with these articles, one can read how the good life amounted to "boating, fishing, or just sitting in the Nevada sun."[22]

Articles championing the excellent fishing in the recreation area's waters also appeared frequently in large-market newspapers during the early to mid-1960s. Whether in search of bass or trout, *Los Angeles Times* journalists assured readers that Lake Mohave and Lake Mead were the places to go. Playing off of southern Nevada's other noted tourist activities, the writers promised anglers that they were sure to "hit [the] jackpot" and find "good action" in their fishing pursuits.[23]

The river below Boulder Dam became known particularly during the era for trophy rainbow trout. This was due in part to state and federal government stocking efforts that dated back to 1945. In May of that year, federal agencies released ten thousand rainbows into the waters between the dam and El Dorado Canyon. During the following January, the Nevada Fish and Game Commission released an additional 100,000 trout there. Before release, the trout were placed in a special "rearing pond" in El Dorado Canyon for four months of growth.[24] *Sunset Magazine's Sportsman's Atlas* for 1952 highlighted the abundance of trophy rainbows caught by fishermen below the dam. The atlas went on to draw attention to the variety of boating options available, including hunting and rock hounding within the recreation area's boundaries.[25]

Fish stocking thus underwrote much of the widely reported success of recreational fishing in the area and its growing popularity. Stocking activities received a boost in March 1962 with the opening of the federally supported Willow Beach National Fish Hatchery just upriver of the Willow Beach recreational facilities. This site offered a prime setting for raising trout due to cold-water releases from the upstream dam. Congressional appropriations funded its construction and operation under the administration of the U.S. Fish and Wildlife Service.[26]

Within two years of its opening, the hatchery was producing approximately one million fish annually for stocking Lake Mohave and stretches of the Colorado River from Needles to Davis Dam and from Lees Ferry to Glen Canyon Dam. Trout fishing in the recreation area during these early years was wildly productive, with numerous trophy-size fish being reported. In one instance, in 1966, an angler landed a record 21 lb. 5 oz. rainbow.[27]

Certainly throughout the 1960s such recreational opportunities continued to attract the attention of popular media writers, which likely drew more recreationists. For example, in 1964 *Arizona Highways* again featured the area and its water-centered opportunities for fun. In his article, Raymond

Carlson proclaimed that Lake Mead and Lake Mohave "offered any warm weather outdoor recreation that people can desire." He also commented on the crowding and popularity of the recreation area. Carlson noted that some three million recreationists had visited LMNRA in 1964. Along with the crowds, he observed that amenities and infrastructure within the area had been upgraded dramatically over the past few years.[28]

NPS-produced media during the period also played a vital role in establishing the area's recreational credentials and in setting the public's expectations. Pamphlets produced from the 1940s through the 1960s are particularly valuable in detecting the NPS's emphasis regarding the area and usage. Specifically, they tended to stress the area's accessibility, amenities, and economy of use.

"Free" was certainly a keyword in many of the NPS-published materials for LMNRA throughout this era. A 1940 pamphlet titled "Boulder Dam National Recreation Area: Arizona and Nevada" highlighted "free facilities" such as diving platforms and dressing rooms.[29] The next year, a much lengthier guide to the area listed "free" motion pictures, museums, swimming, and use of numerous recreation-related amenities under its "What to Do" heading.[30] This emphasis on affordable recreation continued throughout the 1950s, particularly with regard to fishing and boating.

A 1956 guidebook listed long-term mooring as the only charge associated with boating and the state-required license as the only fee for fishing.[31] Five years later, a 1961 pamphlet contained an entirely new section titled "Recreation Facilities." This section listed "Free Facilities" and "Concessioner Facilities" for each section of the recreation area. Under "Free Facilities," one could find both facilities and activities listed. These included swimming, boat docks, boat-launching ramps, and campgrounds. The pamphlet also listed the free amenities at campgrounds. There, one could find comfort stations, water hydrants, shade trees, tables, and fireplaces. Each campground was intended to be "an attractive oasis."[32] By 1964, the "Free" section of the NPS pamphlets had taken on the form of a prominent chart listing the more numerous "Free Facilities" alongside the less numerous "Concession Facilities."[33]

The NPS pamphlets and guidebooks similarly stressed the varied opportunities available at the recreation area. Each pamphlet included narrative and photographic coverage of recreational activities. The 1940 pamphlet provided images of sailing, canoeing, fishing, and motorboating, with captions that read "Thrills for Fishermen" and "Water Sports are Many and Varied."[34] The next year, prospective visitors found images of men landing trophy fish and a narrative describing Lake Mead as offering "the finest bass fishing anywhere in the West."[35] By 1956, the reservoir's water was described as "ideal for swimming," and campgrounds were shown to be very comfortable, with complimentary electric hotplates available for frying up the day's catch.[36] And finally, by 1964, the "unexcelled" motorboating at Lake Mead had become the perfect "family sport."[37]

Throughout much of this era, such family sports were undertaken without excessive regulation at the recreation area. For the most part, regulations and limitations placed on recreational activities seemed limited to state policies that were very general and increasingly oriented toward safety.

The only thing resembling regulation or limitation on activity listed in the 1940 pamphlet was the mention of the state fishing license requirement.[38] The 1941 pamphlet contained a short section titled "Rules and Regulations" that listed applicable restrictions by activity type and was a little more than a page long. Most rules were general and not very prohibitive or intrusive. For example, dogs were "not permitted to run loose," and it was suggested that "people should be quiet after others have gone to bed." Destruction of public property was prohibited, and automobile campers should camp in designated campgrounds unless their distance from such an area made doing so impossible. The only activity specifically prohibited within the area was hunting. Overall, these early regulations seemed to have been aimed at promoting "the comfort, convenience, and safety of visitors."[39]

By 1956, listed regulations stressed accessibility far more than any restrictions on activities. For example, the section on boating stated, "Boats may be launched on Lake Mead at any time." Likewise, fishing was permitted "all day, every day of the year." The earlier ban on hunting had also eased by this time. It was now "permitted" throughout the area "except in certain public use areas." In this regard, a special note was included to stress how open and accessible the recreation area was relative to other NPS units. "Hunting," it read, was "not permitted in other areas administered by the NPS."[40]

In regard to water sports in general, the NPS saw fit to include a somewhat lengthy listing under the heading "Safety Rules." Again, these rules and regulations were what many likely considered standard water safety provisions. Compliance was "urged." In full, the "Safety Rules" stated:

1. Always leave word with someone as to when and where you are going and when you expect to return. This information will aid rescue parties in the event you are missing.
2. Stay ashore when water is rough. If you are on the lake when it is very rough, find a sheltered cove and wait for calm water.
3. Sit down, and sit still when in a boat.
4. Equip your boat with air tanks; carry a life preserver for every passenger; carry day and night flares for use if in distress.
5. Swim only in designated places.[41]

It is of note that one photograph in the same publication showed individuals to be violating rule 3 by standing in a motorboat that was underway. Furthermore, text in the pamphlet promoted swimming along undeveloped shoreline as a recreational opportunity at the park, in seeming violation of rule 5.[42] One has to question how seriously the NPS itself was taking these "rules."

By the 1960s, regulation of activity in the area had become a bit more stringent, at least in some aspects. In terms of safety, the 1961 guide covered the same five "rules" as the 1956 version, although they were recast as "Safety Tips," and the addition of four more tips increased the total to nine. New tips "urged" visitors to be aware that

1. All boats have a load limit. Your boat should not be loaded beyond this capacity.
2. Boats should not be overpowered, especially on rough waters.
3. When traveling off designated roads, carry sufficient water and food supplies.
4. Weather forecasts are available daily at park ranger stations or at offices of concessioners.[43]

Also, the 1961 guide mentioned for the first time the importance of respecting historical artifacts throughout the area: "Digging or disturbing any site or the collecting of items found on the surface is not permitted," as such items were "protected by the Antiquities Act of 1906."[44]

Other examples of increased stringency in the 1960s included a new regulation on skin diving in 1964, which stated that skin divers could not dive along swimming beaches. And two more safety tips were added, bringing the total to eleven.

1. Read all rules and regulations posted at ranger stations, visitor centers, and on bulletin boards.
2. National Park Service Rangers and U.S. Coast Guard Mobile Boarding Teams are stationed at the Lake Mead National Recreation Area to assist boaters and enforce safe boating practices. Your cooperation is appreciated.[45]

The second of the two new safety tips was significant in that it contained the first mention of enforcement of regulations in any guidebook or pamphlet. Such regulations and their enforcement were still, nonetheless, aimed at maintaining a safe recreational environment rather than restricting or limiting recreational activities. This increased emphasis on visitor safety by the mid-1960s is further evident in a section new to the 1964 NPS pamphlets that year. This segment, following "Tips for Your Safety," was titled "Ground-Air Emergency Codes" and provided readers with appropriate ground-to-air signals and instructions for their use. It was noted that these came from the Air Force Survival Manual.[46]

To make the recreation area even more inviting, the NPS also encouraged concessionaires to provide services, goods, and amenities for the recreating public. This was by no means a new or innovative practice, as private companies had done so in all parks since the establishment of Yellowstone National Park in 1872. In fact, the Yellowstone Park Act itself specifically allowed the Secretary of the Interior to lease certain lands within the park for visitor accommodation.[47] This idea was reinforced with the passage of the Organic Act in 1916. In addition to creating the NPS, the Organic Act directly addressed the issue of concessionaires within parklands. Section three echoed the Yellowstone Park Act by specifically allowing for the leasing of national park lands for the accommodation of tourists. After all, both acts listed the primary roles of national parks as both protecting the areas and making them available for public enjoyment. Acknowledging the need for concessionaires certainly stood as a nod toward the latter mandate.[48]

Given that in the new recreation area public enjoyment clearly assumed a primary role, private concessionaires played an equally important role in its growth. From the 1930s to the 1960s, for example, concessionaires such as Grand Canyon-Boulder Dam Tours, Continental Hotel Systems, the Lake Mead Boating Company, Desert Highways, Murl Emery, and E. R. Flother were instrumental in providing tourist amenities and building recreational

FIGURE 3.3. National Park Service boat *NPS No. 1* on reservoir, 1939. Courtesy of
National Park Service Historic Photograph Collection, photographer George A. Grant.

infrastructure.[49] Concessionaires also worked to increase visitation through
advertising and access campaigns. In a late 1930s example, Grand Canyon-
Boulder Dam Tours lobbied for and sponsored airport facility upgrades to
convince Trans World Airlines to fly into Boulder City Airport.[50]

By the 1950s such NPS and private enterprises coincided with changing
American recreational habits to draw record numbers of visitors to LMNRA,
aided by Americans' ever-increasing use of the automobile. Automobile
vacationing had gained significant popularity with the American public by
the time Boulder Dam was completed in 1936. During the twenties, thirties,
and forties, motorcar tourism spread throughout the various economic
strata of the American population. By 1941, Americans spent $6 billion annu-
ally on such trips. This increased to an estimated $18 billion by 1953. During
the mid-1950s Americans spent between 5 and 8 percent of their annual
income on travel, with approximately half of all Americans taking an annual
vacation. Some 83 percent of Americans did so by car within the continental
U.S. Subsequently, by the 1960s, half of the American states counted tourism
among their three most important sources of revenue. In Nevada, thanks
largely to Boulder Dam and Las Vegas gaming, it was the most important
source.[51]

This significant increase in over-the-road tourism was made possible by America's wholehearted adoption of the automobile and the coinciding improvements in the nation's roadways. Motorcar registration numbers drawn from the century's first half show the rapidity and completeness with which Americans embraced the automobile. At the turn of the century, some 8,000 registered motorcars existed in the United States. By 1910, the number had increased to 468,500, which placed the U.S. at the forefront of worldwide auto mobility. From here the growth in automobile ownership was staggeringly exponential, reaching 2 million by 1915 and 10 million by 1920. Twenty years later, in 1940, some 32 million cars traveled American roadways. The number rose to 40.2 million by 1950 and to 61.4 million by 1960.[52]

Development of LMNRA was squarely within the period of the automobile's increasing influence on American culture. Historian James Flink has labeled the period from 1910 until the early 1960s as the second stage of American automobile consciousness. This period, though dominated by such traumatic episodes as the Great Depression and World War II, witnessed the "idolization of the motorcar and a mass accommodation to auto mobility that transformed American institutions and life ways."[53] Throughout the second half of this period, as automobile tourism became deeply entrenched, the NPS and major media outlets were highlighting the cheap recreational activities readily accessible at LMNRA to a growing population of southwestern urbanites. Ultimately, the NPS, and by association LMNRA, catered to increased demand by embarking on a massive building program to upgrade amenities, accessibility, and traffic flow throughout the entire national park system.

To a degree, one can argue that the NPS—officially founded in 1916— grew up with the automobile. Mt. Rainier, General Grant (later, Kings Canyon), Crater Lake, Glacier, Yosemite, Sequoia, Mesa Verde, and Yellowstone national parks had, in fact, opened themselves to automobile travel prior to the founding of the NPS. Already, by 1916, more visitors arrived at Yellowstone National Park by car than by train. Further, the NPS's largest source of income in its first years derived from automobile admission fees.[54]

The service's first director, Stephen T. Mather, certainly recognized the link between park development, the automobile, and the popular support necessary for adequate congressional funding. To this end, he joined with the automobile interest groups in pressuring Congress for better roadways within the parks. This strategy brought success in 1923, with congressional appropriation of $7.5 million for road building in national parks between 1924 and 1927. Due to the prohibitive expense of road construction in many areas, these funds were directed primarily at grading and widening existing roads.[55]

Contrary to what might be expected, the Great Depression saw a marked upswing in federal road funding and national park road construction. Between 1933 and 1940, New Deal programs pumped $220 million into national park road development. The majority of these funds went to paving existing roads and building scenic parkways. Yet large as it was, this amount was miniscule in comparison to the $4 billion the FDR administrations spent to improve roads and highways throughout the Depression in its work-relief efforts.[56]

By the outbreak of World War II, national park visitation had grown to approximately 17 million per year. The war brought a temporary dip in visitation and road development, and the NPS budget plummeted from $21 million annually to $5 million by 1943. In 1941, a record 20.5 million people visited national parks. That number decreased to 8.9 million for 1942 and a wartime low of 6.4 million for 1943. Yet, after the war ended, visitation quickly surpassed previous records. Some 22 million visitors arrived at the parks in 1946. A whopping 48 million visited in 1954.[57] Yet budgeting for the parks and for park enhancements remained stagnant throughout the 1950s. Park infrastructure subsequently became outdated and overwhelmed.[58] Further, with the dismantling of New Deal programs such as the CCC and Public Works Administration (PWA) in the early 1940s, the NPS lost a very important resource for road and amenity construction. Thus, as visitation was increasing due to the automobile, the NPS found itself increasingly unable to handle the influx.[59]

Local visitation numbers at LMNRA reflected the overwhelming trend evident in national park statistics. Prior to U.S. entry into World War II, recreational visits to LMNRA had increased steadily from 389,294 in 1936 to 844,773 in 1941, a respectable 117 percent growth. Then, following Pearl Harbor, visitation declined markedly. In 1942, only 338,320 recreationists visited the park. Wartime visitation bottomed out at 214,190 people for 1943, and grew only slightly to 263,533 for 1944. This wartime decline reflects the concurrent militarization of LMNRA. During the war, military personnel controlled area access and guarded the dam as a vital national interest. Training exercises were conducted in the immediate vicinity, and the government used recreation area resources for war industry development. With the war's end in 1945, such use waned, and recreational visitation quickly surpassed prewar levels. By 1946, over a million recreationists were visiting each year. Within ten years, more than 2.5 million were visiting annually.[60] By that time, the recreation area ranked second in annual visitation among the 181 NPS-administered units. Only Great Smoky Mountains National Park hosted more people on a yearly basis.[61]

Dramatic population growth in surrounding areas, which supplied a large portion of area visitors, had combined with increased auto mobility and better roadways to account for such significant growth. Los Angeles County's population, for example, grew from 2.7 million to 4.1 million from 1940 to 1950. In Nevada, Clark County's population likewise increased from 16,414 to 48,289 over the same period. These burgeoning populations were among the most automobile-oriented in the world. By the early 1950s, California residents registered more automobiles than any other state.[62]

With the monumental Federal Highway Act of 1956, the U.S. government promised to add to LMNRA's and the NPS's already dire situation by stimulating further exponential increase in visitation. Through this act, the federal government committed to pay 90 percent of construction costs for the development of 41,000 miles of interstate highways to be completed by June 30, 1976.[63] Faced with the increase in visitation that such a road system would likely create, the NPS had to come up with an innovative way to secure the massive funding required for large-scale park development.

The solution came from NPS Director Conrad Wirth. He reasoned that controlled development of roadways, visitor centers, and lodging within the parks' boundaries could accomplish both goals effectively. By improving visitor amenities in certain areas of the parks, the NPS could direct the visitation flow to those areas and thus relieve pressure on undeveloped landscapes. Further, he believed that this undertaking should be designed as a nationwide, multiyear, congressionally funded program that would be of long-term benefit to congressional districts across the nation.[64]

Wirth presented the idea of a ten-year park improvement plan to President Dwight Eisenhower at a January 1956 cabinet meeting. Impressed with the need for such action, Eisenhower placed his full support behind Wirth's plan. Less than a month later, the president formally announced the Mission 66 program during a banquet address at the nation's capital. Secretary of the Interior Douglas McKay and leaders of the American Automobile Association joined Wirth and Eisenhower in publicly supporting the program. With congressional and powerful special-interest support, the $785 million program began on July 1, 1956.[65]

Under the Mission 66 guidelines, the NPS set out to modernize facilities and prepare infrastructure to accommodate 80 million visitors per year by 1966. Plans included extensive construction of roads, trails, parking areas, water systems, sewer systems, administrative buildings, employee houses, refurbished and reconstructed historical structures, and visitor centers. Landscape architects, under the supervision of NPS Chief Landscape Architect William Carnes, developed extensive master plans for each park. In conceptualizing these plans, the architects were instructed to keep the new structures somewhat humble, so as not to dominate their surroundings.[66]

This conservative approach to park design was likely an acknowledgment of the degree of controversy Mission 66 created among some segments of the public. Several of the nation's most established preservationist groups, for example, opposed the program. Organizations such as the Sierra Club and the Wilderness Society maintained that Mission 66's "bulldozers of bureaucracy" would despoil and degrade the national parks' pristine or exceptional wilderness settings. To many of the program's opponents, the idea of new roads, accommodations, and visitor centers smacked of the urbanization, modernization, and overdevelopment of the national parks.[67]

Mission 66 also upset traditionalists with its prescribed architectural style. The new structures tended to eschew the rustic, log-cabin style normally employed in national park settings. In place of rough-hewn logs, Mission 66 architects preferred the concrete and straight lines of modernist and functional designs. This preference was influenced by the fact that many of the Mission 66 architects had trained after World War II, worked for the Bureau of Reclamation on utilitarian dam designs, and had served as military architects in the preceding years. Further, modern designs and modern building materials were cheaper and required less upkeep than did the more traditional. Yet, where the rustic designs had celebrated wilderness and the frontier, the modernist structures brought forth urban associations.[68]

Regardless of such criticism, the Mission 66 program enjoyed widespread acclaim, particularly among other federal agencies. Shortly following the program's implementation, other resource-oriented federal services looked

FIGURE 3.4. The Mission 66–era, Alan Bible Visitor Center at Lake Mead National Recreation Area, 2010. Courtesy of Marianne Molland.

to copy the NPS success and implement their own ten-year plans. In 1957 alone, both the Fish and Wildlife Service and the Forest Service moved to produce similar multiyear development programs.[69]

If the goal was simply to increase access, these agencies had good reason to copy the NPS program. In its first three years, Mission 66 accounted for some 1,946 projects within the NPS units. Federal money provided for these projects amounted to $96.4 million. By 1960, hundreds of miles of service roadways and over 100 miles of visitor parkways had been completed within the parks, over 10,000 new campsites built, hundreds of miles of new hiking trails cleared, and more than thirty new visitor centers had either been completed or were under construction. Mission 66 goals of 1,500 miles of new trails, 300 miles of visitor parkways, and the construction of 100 new visitor centers by the program's termination date of 1966 seemed well within reach.[70]

From the recreationists' viewpoint, Mission 66 provided many sorely needed upgrades. At LMNRA, Mission 66 planners focused on enhanced access and accommodations for tourists, plus increased recreational amenities. These projects included expanding and updating facilities associated with boating, swimming, fishing, and camping, improving roadways, building new visitor and ranger stations, and expanding park concessionaire facilities.[71]

It is significant that the controversies over Mission 66 seem to have been largely absent for LMNRA. That Mission 66 did not elicit such opposition in the local or national media indicates that the public's concept of NRAs differed from their perception of national parks. Even as both were part of the national park system and overseen by the same NPS, NRAs simply did not enjoy the same protectionist sentiment as national parks when it came to changes in the landscape or increased access. To the contrary, as became evident in decades after the 1960s, the public's primary protectionist sentiments toward the recreation areas were centered on accessibility and availability of a group's chosen recreational activity.

While the popular press and NPS worked toward defining the recreation area in terms of usage from the 1930s to the 1960s, the U.S. Government moved toward a political definition of national recreation areas. This was a slow process, where the government gradually realized the importance of outdoor recreation and ultimately defined a system of national recreation areas based on the LMNRA model.

The government's increased awareness of the importance of outdoor recreation and its own role in providing it can be seen as early as 1942. That year, Secretary of the Interior Ickes wrote in the foreword to the NPS's "Study of the Park and Recreation Problem of the United States" that the nation's need for outdoor recreational outlets remained "pertinent" and must be addressed even during wartime. He further asserted that "participation in recreational activities is vital to the welfare of the people, both military and civilian."[72]

The report mentioned above originated from the NPS's Park, Parkway, and Recreational Area Study, initiated in June 1937. With its stated objective of establishing "a basis for coordinated, correlated recreation land planning among all agencies," this study's purpose reflected New Deal tendencies toward centralized planning.[73] More importantly, it reflected the increased recognition of outdoor recreation and need for government attention to its availability.

Whereas the interagency agreement of 1937 and the national recreation area it created met some of that need, it was obvious by the late 1940s that it did not go far enough. Most obviously, a lone national recreation area no longer met present or future demands. It did not set a path for the creation of other areas and failed to adequately address the specifics of the existing one. Yet, the memorandum of agreement remained the basis for the national recreation area's existence for twenty-eight years. Over time, the ill-defined marriage of convenience of the USBR and NPS grew problematic. As early as 1945, issues concerning expansion of the recreation area's boundaries and disagreement over its main purpose led the NPS to push for revision of the agreement and more independence from the USBR in the area's management. In 1947, a new agreement between the USBR and NPS provided for the transfer of the area surrounding the as-yet incomplete Davis Dam and its prospective reservoir to the recreation area and NPS control. At that time the Boulder Dam Recreation Area became known as the Lake Mead National Recreation Area (LMNRA), a name made official in 1964. As historian Hal Rothman points out, this name change subtly moved the emphasis of the park away from the dam and indirectly advanced the idea of a recreation area with greater independence from the USBR.[74]

Still, the cooperation between the USBR and NPS in regard to the area's management stands as one of the most significant aspects in the national recreation area's creation and existence. Historian Douglas Dodd has argued that this cooperation was beneficial to both entities but ultimately damaging to the preservationist cause. In this regard, the USBR had managed to focus on water control, and the NPS managed to enlarge its holdings and take a more active role in the nation's recreational management. Cooperation between the two entities concerning Boulder Dam and the recreation area allowed the USBR to more easily proceed with more controversial dam-building projects such as Echo Park and Glen Canyon. If cracks in the marriage were appearing by the 1940s and 1950s, it was only after more than a decade of at least tolerable and mutually productive cohabitation.[75]

In the period that followed, the NPS's role in overseeing the national recreation area finally received official sanction and definition. The facilitating chain of events further reflected the government's growing perception of a demand for more outdoor recreation sites. In 1958, for example, Congress created the Outdoor Recreation Resources Review Commission (ORRRC). Its 1960 report underlined the need for more government involvement in outdoor recreation and recommended creation of a Bureau of Outdoor Recreation within the Department of Interior to oversee and coordinate federal recreation policy.[76] The commission also listed an urgent need for additional NRAs to be created in close proximity to large urban areas. It went on to estimate that the already heavy demand for outdoor recreation would increase threefold by the year 2000.[77]

By the 1960s, with demands for outdoor recreational access to public lands mushrooming, a somewhat "neopopulist" idea of "parks for people, where the people are" had gained traction.[78] This reflected the increased recreation-consciousness of a greatly urbanized society with more leisure time, disposable income, and exposure to mass communication advertising. By 1959, outdoor recreation had also emerged as a major industry, with Americans spending approximately $18 billion per year on outdoor recreational pursuits. National parks were bearing much of the weight of this postwar growth, evidenced by the 133 million visits to national parks in 1960. The increasing popularity of outdoor recreation and changing social values led to apocalyptic predictions from some academics that future recreational demand would increase exponentially and uncontrollably. Professor Raleigh Barlowe of Michigan State University, for example, argued that decreases in working hours and affluence, plus an increase in population, would result in a fifteenfold increase in demand for recreational outlets by the year 2000.[79] When viewed in such context, it is not surprising that the government moved to make the national recreation system official and begin its rapid expansion in the early 1960s.

This long developmental phase of the national recreation area culminated with the federal government's defining of recreation areas in 1963. That year, the President's Recreation Advisory Council officially created a national recreation area system with the "Policy on the Establishment and Administration of Recreation Areas." This policy defined a "system of National Recreation Areas" whose "dominant or primary purpose" was meeting the "steeply mounting outdoor recreation demands of the American people." It also established seven primary and six secondary criteria for NRA designation. The criteria required NRAs to be spacious and close to urban areas. NRAs were to place outdoor recreation as their primary resource management activity while prohibiting any resource utilization detrimental to such recreational opportunities. Additional language required that NRA landscapes and natural settings be above ordinary in quality but below what is required for designation as a national park and allowed for the cultural management of "historic, scientific, scarce, or disappearing resources," as long as such preservation activities were "compatible with the recreation mission."[80]

This was a recreation-first mandate that sought to bring outdoor recreation to an increasingly urban population. One cannot help but see its basis in the preexisting characteristics of the urban-accessible LMNRA. It is difficult and, to a degree, unfair to fault the government for developing such criteria in the image of LMNRA at that time. From 1936 to 1963, LMNRA had certainly exhibited striking success in providing residents of Las Vegas, Los Angeles, Phoenix, and the greater Southwest with recreational opportunities and enjoyment. Throughout this period, the NPS consistently acted to provide LMNRA visitors with cheap, open access and largely unregulated recreational activities. From their own publicity efforts to Mission 66, the NPS's actions planted such expectations in the minds of LMNRA visitors. In this regard, the NPS had been strikingly successful during LMNRA's first three decades of existence.

But in many instances, visitor beliefs grown during those times have not evolved along with drastic changes in the wider historical context since then. In subsequent years, the NPS has faced incredible challenges as it has attempted to adapt its management and public usage of NRAs to rapid changes in post-1960s America. During this era, the NPS has struggled to meet the public's water-based recreational expectations at an increasingly urbanized and arid region's primary reservoir.

NOTES

1. "198 CCC Boys in B.C. to Begin Park Projects," *Las Vegas Evening Review-Journal,* 11 November 1935; "Boulder CCC Camp Now Numbers 500," *Las Vegas Evening Review-Journal,* 16 January 1936; "CCC To Cease In Boulder City Next Tuesday," *Boulder City News,* 23 July 1942.

2. "Closing out of CCC Program Complete Work Revisited," *Boulder City News,* 28 August 1942; "Bad Wash-Out Caused by Cloudburst," *Boulder City Reminder,* 13 September 1939.

3. "Bathing Beach at Dam Lake is Being Built," *Las Vegas Evening Review-Journal,* 8 April 1936; Guy D. Edwards, "Lake Recreational Development Carried on By CCC," *Las Vegas Evening Review-Journal,* 22 April 1936; "Closing Out of CCC Program Complete Work Revisited," *Boulder City News,* 28 August 1942.

4. Guy D. Edwards, "Lake Recreational Development Carried on By CCC," *Las Vegas Evening Review-Journal,* 22 April 1936; "Closing Out of CCC Program Complete Work Reviewed," *Boulder City News,* 28 August 1942; J.C. Reddoch, "Supplementary Report: Camp SP-6, Company 2536, Boulder City, Nevada," 5 February 1937; Earl W. Banister, "Active Work Projects: Camp NP–6, Boulder City, Nevada," 28 September 1938; Box Civilian Conservation Corps (CCC) Nevada: Camp Inspection Reports, Folder Civilian Conservation Corps (CCC)—Nevada: Boulder City, Nevada, 1935–1941, Camp No. NP–6. UNLVSPC; "Landscaping of B.C. Building Begun," *Las Vegas Evening Review-Journal,* 18 February 1938; "Geological and Wild Life Survey At Dam

Started," *Las Vegas Evening Review-Journal,* 29 April 1936; "Tourist-checking Stations at Dam Planned," *Las Vegas Evening Review-Journal,* 25 February 1937; "Tourist Checking Stations Start Thursday Morn," *Las Vegas Evening Review-Journal,* 31 March 1937.

5. Douglas Dodd, "Boulder Dam Recreation Area: The Bureau of Reclamation, the National Park Service, and the Origins of the National Recreation Area Concept at Lake Mead, 1929–1936," in *The Bureau of Reclamation: History Essays from the Centennial Symposium,* edited by Brit Allan Storey, Denver: U.S. Bureau of Reclamation, 2008.

6. Ibid., 485–86.

7. Russell K. Grater, "The Story of Davis Dam," *Arizona Highways,* March 1956, 8, 12.

8. Ibid., 8, 11–12; "Interior Department Approves Proposed $41,200,000 Dam," *Los Angeles Times,* 29 April 1941.

9. Secretary Ickes quoted in "Interior Department Approves Proposed $41,200,000 Dam," *Los Angeles Times,* 29 April 1941.

10. Ibid.; "Letter From the Acting Secretary of the Interior Transmitting the Reclamation Report on the Bulls Head Dam Project on the Colorado River Where that Stream Forms the Boundary Between Arizona and Nevada," 77th Congress, House of Representatives, Doc. No. 186, April 28, 1941. (Hereafter, Bulls Head Dam Project Report).

11. James E. Bassett Jr. "Davis Dam, Fourth in Colorado Chain, Promises Rich Development," *Los Angeles Times,* 23 April 1946.

12. Ibid.; "Huge Dam Project Nears Its Halfway Mark," *Los Angeles Times,* 7 June 1948; "Colorado River Diverted for Construction of Davis Dam," *Los Angeles Times,* 28 June 1948; "Davis Dam to Impound Water Late this Week," *Los Angeles Times,* 29 November 1949; "Davis Dam Ready on Colorado River," *New York Times,* 4 December 1949; "Davis Dam Almost Ready," *Los Angeles Times,* 19 December 1950; "Davis Dam Open Friday," *New York Times,* 2 January 1951; "Davis Dam Power Use Starts Friday," *Los Angeles Times,* 2 January 1951; "Dedication Set for Davis Dam," *Los Angeles Times,* 28 November 1952; "Governors Due at Dam Rites," *Los Angeles Times,* 3 December 1952.

13. Hal Rothman, "Administrative History of the Lake Mead National Recreation Area," unpublished manuscript in author's possession, 263–64.

14. Alexander Gardiner, "Out of the Desert: An Empire," *American Legion Monthly,* December 1934, 18–21, 48–50.

15. United States Bureau of Reclamation, "Construction of Boulder Dam," Washington, D.C.: Department of the Interior, no publication date (1930s).

16. Boulder Dam Post Card Booklet, Chicago: Curt Teich & Co., 1935.

17. U.S. Postal Service, Three-Cent Stamp, 1935.

18. Gordon C. Baldwin, "The Lake Becomes a Playground," *Arizona Highways,* July 1946, 25.

19. TWA Advertisement, "The Joy's in the Journey," 1946 (advertisement in author's possession).

20. U.S. Bureau of Reclamation, "Boulder Dam," pamphlet, Washington, D.C.: Department of the Interior, 1940s.

21. Charley Niehus, "Fishing in Lake Mead and Lake Mohave," *Arizona Highways,* March 1956, 4–7.

22. "Stopover in Sunland," *Nevada Highways,* no. 1, 1961, 18–25.

23. Lupi Saldana, "Anglers Hit Jackpot: Trout, Bass Bagged on Colorado River," *Los Angeles Times,* 26 March 1965; "Trout, Bass Action Moves Into High Gear," *Los Angeles Times,* 23 April 1965; "Fresh Water Fishing," *Los Angeles Times,* 10 December 1965; "Trout, Bass Share Spotlight," *Los Angeles Times,* 19 March 1966; "River to Get Big Plants of 8-Inch Trout," *Los Angeles Times,* 15 April 1966.

24. "100,000 Baby Trout Put to Bed, To Be Planted in River in January," *Boulder City News,* 19 September 1945.

25. C. E. Erikson, *Sunset Sportsman's Atlas: Colorado River and Lake Mead: Boating, Fishing, Exploring* (Menlo Park: Lane Publishing, 1952), 2–5.

26. John Kimak, "Fishing for Answers from Willow Beach Hatchery," *Las Vegas Review-Journal,* 1 August 1996; U.S. Fish and Wildlife Service, "Willow Beach National Fish Hatchery," http://www.fws.gov/SOUTHWEST/fisheries/willow_beach/index.html (accessed February 5, 2016); Margo Bartlett Pesek, "Trip of the Week: Willow Beach Fish Hatchery Offers Educational Trip," *Las Vegas Review-Journal,* 17 April 2005.

27. John Kimak, "Rainbow Trout Production Resumes at Arizona Hatchery," *Las Vegas Review-Journal,* 19 January 2003; Kimak, "Fishing for Answers from Willow Beach Hatchery."

28. Raymond Carlson, "The Blue Waters of Lake Mead and Mohave," *Arizona Highways,* May 1964, 1–2.

29. U.S. Department of the Interior, National Park Service, "Boulder Dam National Recreation Area: Arizona and Nevada," September, 1940. (Hereafter: NPS, "BDNRA: Arizona and Nevada," 1940.)

30. U.S. Department of the Interior, National Park Service, "Boulder Dam National Recreation Area: Arizona and Nevada," Denver: W. H. Kistler Stationery Company, March, 1941, 13–15. (Hereafter: NPS, "BDNRA: Arizona and Nevada." 1941.)

31. U.S. Department of the Interior, National Park Service, "Lake Mead National Recreation Area: Lake Mead and Lake Mohave," Washington: U.S. Government Printing Office, 1956, 12–13. (Hereafter: NPS, "LMNRA: Lake Mead and Lake Mohave," 1956.)

32. U.S. Department of the Interior, National Park Service, "Lake Mead National Recreation Area: Arizona and Nevada: Lake Mead and Lake Mohave," Washington: U.S. Government Printing Office, 1961, 8–11. (Hereafter: NPS, "LMNRA: Lake Mead and Mohave," 1961).

33. U.S. Department of the Interior, National Park Service, "Lake Mead National Recreation Area: Mohave-Arizona and Nevada-Lake Mead," Washington: U.S. Government Printing Office, 1964, 5. (Hereafter: NPS, "LMNRA: Mohave-Mead," 1964).

34. NPS, "BDNRA: Arizona and Nevada," 1940.

35. NPS, "BDNRA: Arizona and Nevada," 1941, 15.

36. NPS, "LMNRA: Lake Mead and Lake Mohave," 1956, 9–10.

37. NPS, "LMNRA: Mohave-Mead," 1964, 3.

38. NPS, "BDNRA: Arizona and Nevada," 1940.

39. NPS, "BDNRA: Arizona and Nevada," 1941,16.

40. NPS, "LMNRA: Lake Mead and Lake Mohave," 1956, 13–15.

41. Ibid., 16–17.

42. Ibid., 5–6, 12.

43. NPS, "LMNRA: Lake Mead and Mohave," 1961, 20–21.

44. Ibid., 14.

45. NPS, "LMNRA: Mohave-Mead," 1964, 4–5.

46. Ibid., 5.

47. Richard West Sellars, *Preserving Nature in the National Parks: A History* (New Haven: Yale University Press), 19.

48. Ibid., 44; Yellowstone Park Act, March 1, 1972 (17 Stat. 32); National Park Service Organic Act of 1916 (16 U.S.C. l 2 3, and 4), August 25, 1916 (39 Stat. 535).

49. Sellars, *Preserving Nature*, 131–33.

50. McBride, "Grand Canyon-Boulder Dam Tours, Inc.," 102–03; National Park Service, "Meadview Area History," http://www. nps.gov/lake/historyculture/meadview history.htm (accessed April 30, 2010).

51. John B. Rae, *The Road and the Car in American Life* (Cambridge: MIT Press, 1971), 138–42.

52. James J. Flink, "Three Stages of Automobile Consciousness," *American Quarterly* 24 (October 1972):454; Rae, *The Road and the Car in American Life,* 38, 49–50.

53. Flink, "Three Stages of Automobile Consciousness," 452.

54. Flink, *The Automobile Age* (Cambridge: MIT Press, 1990), 172–73.

55. Ibid.

56. Ibid., 174–75.

57. National Park Service, "Annual Summary Report," https://irma.nps.gov/Stats /SSRSReports/National%20Reports/Annual%20Summary%20Report%20%281 904%20-%20Last%20Calendar%20Year%29 (accessed February 6, 2016).

58. Flink, *The Automobile Age,* 175.

59. Ethan Carr, *Mission 66: Modernism and the National Park Dilemma* (Amherst: University of Massachusetts Press, 2007), 1–5.

60. National Park Service, "Lake Mead NRA: Annual Park Recreation Visitation," https://irma.nps.gov/Stats/SSRSReports/Park Specific Reports/Annual Park Recrea tion Visitation (1904 - Last Calendar Year)?Park=LAKE; Eugene P. Moehring, "Las Vegas and the Second World War," *Nevada Historical Society Quarterly* 29 (spring 1986):1–2; "Visitors Banned From Power Plant at Boulder Dam," *Las Vegas Evening Review-Journal,* 8 December 1941; Andrew J. Dunbar and Dennis McBride, *Building Hoover Dam: An Oral History of the Great Depression* (New York: Twayne Publishers, 1993), 299.

61. Flink, *The Automobile Age,* 15, 18.

62. Elaine Jackson-Retondo, "National Register of Historic Places Multiple Property Documentation Form, Lake Mead National Recreation Area Mission 66 Resources" (Oakland: National Park Service, Pacific West Region, 2007), 14–15.

63. Flink, *The Automobile Age,* 175–76.

64. Sellars, *Preserving Nature,* 181–83.

65. Ibid., 183; Carr, *Mission 66,* 10; John B. Oates, "Conservation: The Ten Year Plan," *New York Times,* 4 March 1956; William M. Blair, "Saving the Parks," *New York Times,* 12 February 1956; "Mission 66," *New York Times,* 26 February 1956; "Progress Noted In Park Program," *New York Times,* 4 December 1960.

66. Ibid., 183–84; M. Guy Bishop, "Mission 66 in the National Parks of Southern California and the Southwest," *Southern California Quarterly* 80 (fall 1998):294.

67. Sierra Club quoted in Carr, "Mission 66," 228; Sellars, *Preserving Nature,* 186, 188; Bishop, "Mission 66," 294; "Mr. Wirth's Departure," *New York Times,* 24 January 1964.

68. Sellars, *Preserving Nature,* 185–87.

69. John B. Oates, "Conservation: Long-Term Plans," *New York Times,* 7 April 1957.

70. "Chief Says Parks Get Best of Care," *New York Times,* 30 August 1930; Jay Walz, "Park Service Lists Gains," *New York Times,* 10 November 1957; Jay Walz, "U.S. Parks' Gains," *New York Times,* 9 March 1958; Mary Frances Loftus, "Making The Parks More Fit," *New York Times,* 7 June 1959; "Progress Noted In Park Program," *New York Times,* 4 December 1960; William M. Blair, "Saving the Parks," *New York Times,* 12 February 1956.

71. Bishop, "Mission 66 in the National Parks of Southern California and the Southwest," 303–06; Jackson-Retondo, "National Register of Historic Places Multiple Property Documentation Form, Lake Mead National Recreation Area Mission 66 Resources," 18.

72. National Park Service, Department of the Interior, "A Study of the Park and Recreation Problem of the United States," Washington: Government Printing Office, 1941, supplemental foreword.

73. Ibid., foreword.

74. National Park Service, "Lake Mead: Historic Timeline," https://www.nps.gov/lake/learn/news/timeline.htm; Rothman, "Administrative History," 37–38.

75. Dodd, "Boulder Dam Recreation Area," 488.

76. Thomas G. Smith, "John Kennedy, Stewart Udall, and New Frontier Conservation," *Pacific Historical Review* 64 (August 1995):340.

77. H, Ken Cordell and Gregory R. Super, "Trends in America's Outdoor Recreation," in *Trends and Outdoor Recreation, Leisure, and Tourism,* edited by William C. Gartner and David W. Lime (Wallingford, UK: CABI Publishing, 2000):133–34.

78. Hal Rothman, *The New Urban Park: Golden Gate National Recreation Area and Civic Environmentalism* (Lawrence: University Press of Kansas, 2004), ix.

79. Raleigh Barlowe, "Past, Present, and Future Demand for Land for Recreation," *Agricultural History* 36 (October 1962):230.

80. "Policy on the Establishment and Administration of Recreation Areas: Federal Executive Branch Policy Governing the Selection, Establishment, and Administration of National Recreation Areas by the Recreation Advisory Council," Circular 1, March 26, 1963.

CHAPTER FOUR

Balancing Act

Recreation and Modern Challenges at
Lake Mead National Recreation Area, 1967–2000

In the twentieth century's latter decades, LMNRA faced a more difficult existence than it had during its first thirty years, for many of the problems inherent to NPS management of reservoir-based recreation became evident. Despite the improved amenities made possible by Mission 66, area officials faced ever-more difficult challenges in meeting the recreation-first mandate laid out by the government's NRA criteria of 1963. The NPS's management role grew exceedingly difficult as the public's expectations of free, safe, and unregulated recreation ran up against increased crime and accident rates and the conflicting needs of various factions of recreationists, environmentalists, and administrators. This required the NPS and LMNRA administrators to exercise their power of regulation over park activities and accessibility more regularly. Thus, public anxiety mounted as the image of LMNRA and its visitors' experience began to suffer.

In 1967, one year after the Mission 66 program's conclusion, LMNRA hosted 4,102,300 visitors. This statistic indicates an astounding increase in visitation over the recreation area's first thirty years. In 1937, after all, only 389,294 people had visited the newly created recreation area. Though usage increased dramatically during the area's first thirty years of existence, visitation growth over the next thirty years was even more impressive. In 1997, the area admitted some 8.5 million people. This number, nonetheless, was approximately 1.3 million fewer than the 9.8 million who visited in the most popular year of 1995.[1]

The popularity of LMNRA during this era is further underscored by its visitation rankings relative to other NPS units. Over an eleven-year span, from 1989 to 2000, the recreation area ranked in the top five of all NPS units in terms of annual visitation. For four of these years, including the peak year of 1995, LMNRA ranked third.[2]

Such popularity was a doubled-edged sword. Along with accolades for success in attracting visitors, busy administrators and staff often had to deal with inadequate funding and visitation-related problems. Specifically, the NPS and recreation area officials had to provide a safe and accessible setting for an overwhelming flood tide of recreationists, while attempting to preserve the area's unique environment and cultural resources. Navigation of this difficult path often led to tension between competing groups regarding access, regulation, and environmental degradation.

An incident in Yosemite National Park on July 4, 1970, served as a harbinger of the issues to be faced by the NPS and LMNRA during this period. That day, a gathering of some 500 counterculture youths rioted at the park's Stoneman Meadow. Provoked by the attempted arrest of one of their own, youths battled park rangers with rocks and bottles, ransacked campsites, and overturned automobiles. Reports also alleged that rangers opened fire with shotguns before being driven off by the rioters. Rangers returned with reinforcements and regained control of the area the next day. The battle resulted in ninety arrests on charges of drunk and disorderly and minors in possession of alcohol. Approximately thirty rioters and five rangers received medical treatment for injuries.[3]

The incident received much publicity at the time and fostered a perception that parks were getting out of control and dangerous. It also marked the beginning of law enforcement and safety as major issues for the NPS during the 1970s, 1980s, and 1990s.[4,5] Increasingly throughout this period, the NPS had to acknowledge and address visitor safety and criminal activity. At LMNRA, this sharper focus on safety often resulted in a very difficult balancing act, given its recreation-first mandate, well-established public perception of free and lightly regulated recreation, and its proximity to a rapidly growing urban area.

The highly publicized Yosemite Riot also pushed the wheels of government into motion. Recognizing the need for increased emphasis on law enforcement at NPS units, Congress allocated funds for the establishment of a Washington, D.C.–based law-enforcement office, a more intensive training program for rangers, and the rapid deployment of a special U.S. Park Police force to certain parks in the event of disturbances. A government appropriation of $500,000 funded this forty-member "riot control squad." LMNRA was among the group of twelve parks specifically listed as likely deployment sites for the newly created force.[6]

Such high-profile government action, while likely helping to reduce crime, further heightened concern over safety at LMNRA. On the surface, the need for concern certainly seemed strong, as higher visitation levels, more dangerous types of recreational activities, and an extreme setting all worked together to increase the overall number of accident-related fatalities. For example, between 1936 and 1996, accidents claimed 564 lives at LMNRA. Half of these took place over the forty-year span between 1936 and 1976, whereas the second half took only nineteen years to occur.[7] Still, the overall perception that a visit to LMNRA had become more dangerous was mistaken. Looking at the rate of accidents per 100,000 visitors during these two eras, a different picture emerges. While the overall number of deaths by accident increased, the number of visitors increased at a much greater pace. From 1937 to 1976, some 108,724,892 people visited LMNRA. From 1977 to 1997, recreational visits numbered 150,240,242. The accidental death rate for visitors was approximately .26 per 100,000 for the period 1936–1976. From 1977 to 1996, the accidental death rate was approximately .19 per 100,000 visitors.[8] In other words, LMNRA actually became safer for visitors as time passed. While it is likely that increased emphasis on safety and regulation of activities contributed to this declining accident rate, it is also notable that the rate honestly was not very high to begin with. The chances of surviving one's recreation at LMNRA were overwhelmingly favorable.

On the other hand, there was a greater chance of being involved in an incident when boating. It thus comes as no surprise that administrators of the reservoir-based recreation area were quite concerned about boating safety, with an increased emphasis evident as early as 1971. That year, LMNRA implemented regulations on whitewater rafting between Lee's Ferry and Temple Bar. NPS Director George B. Hartzog's expressed reason for doing so was "to protect the wilderness quality of the area and safety of the thousands of people" who engage in such activity.[9]

Twenty years later, in 1991, boating and water safety remained at the forefront of administrators' concerns at LMNRA. A quick look at accident statistics for this period illustrates why. In 1991 alone, boating accidents resulted in fifty-five injuries on the Colorado River reservoirs. Of these, two on Lake Mead and two on Lake Mohave were fatal. These deaths and injuries resulted from a total of 108 boating accidents. In 1992 rangers carried out 242 search-and-rescue missions within the park. Though this number had decreased to 146 by 1998, accidental deaths and boating accidents remained problematic. That year, twenty-five people died accidentally in the recreation area, and boating accidents numbered 136.[10] These numbers earned the Colorado River second place among all U.S. waterways in number of water-related accidents during 1997–2000. Lake Mead alone ranked fifth in this category. [11]

In light of such numbers, and out of increased concern with environmental quality, the NPS moved to regulate boating activities. Specifically, it proposed a general ban on personal watercraft (PWC or jet skis) in 1998. The proposal ignited a national, multiyear debate over proper recreational usage and regulation of NPS lands, and LMNRA became an epicenter of opposition.

Public interest was high in the proposed PWC ban, marked by passionate support and opposition. During the sixty-day comment period following the proposed ban, the NPS received approximately 20,000 responses. Environmentalists, fishermen, and other recreationists seeking a serene, lake-oriented experience supported the ban. To them, the continued use of PWCs threatened both the natural setting and recreational enjoyment.[12] Other recreationists viewed the ban as an assault on their ability to recreate in the manner of their choice.

Irrespective of noise levels and others' concepts of serenity, the idea of PWC regulation at LMNRA drew heavy local criticism. A *Las Vegas Review-Journal* editorial displayed an attitude very much at odds with the NPS regarding regulation of recreational usage. The piece took issue with the idea of leaving possible future regulation to the discretion of the park superintendent. Such individuals, the editor opined, had repeatedly demonstrated that their discretion leaned toward "banning any public use" that they could. Advising local recreationists not to "kid" themselves about the issue, the editorial asserted that the banning of personal watercraft would eventually extend to LMNRA. To boating enthusiasts, any such regulation threatened the recreational freedom they had long enjoyed at LMNRA. Attempting to fan the flames of public outcry against the measure, the editorial further warned of the likelihood that the "federals" would come after their fishing and pleasure boats as well.[13]

The PWC issue would not be settled until the next decade, but the reactions of the various parties involved provides insight into how visitors viewed the area by the late 1990s. By this time, most had only known the area as an expansive reservoir with a recreational orientation. For decades

FIGURE 4.1. Crowds of recreationists at Boulder Beach, Lake Mead National Recreation Area, 2010. Photo by author.

they had enjoyed freedom to fish, swim, boat, and so on largely without interference. However, problems arose as modern technology and heavy visitation resulted in some people's recreational activities conflicting with those of others. Both pro-PWC and anti-PWC activists viewed the reservoir in terms of recreational opportunity. Their difference was merely over the other group's right to interfere with their own opportunity.

The difference points to the development of an environmental values system among recreationists that is rooted in the perceived right to unimpeded exercise of a chosen form of outdoor recreation. As Marc Reisner and Sarah Bates observed in their study, *Overtapped Oasis,* any assessment of the impact of federal water development in the West is dependent upon each group's values. For flat-water fishermen, as an example, reservoirs enhance the environment. Yet the same reservoirs are viewed as degrading the environment by whitewater rafters or stream fly fishermen. Likewise, regulations to prohibit jet skis are welcomed by fishermen and abhorred as overreaching regulation by pleasure boaters.[14]

Beyond such divisions among various recreation area interest groups, concerns over an upsurge in illegal activity within LMNRA's boundaries have shaped the park setting and recreationists' experiences in recent decades.

During this period, LMNRA shared national trends of increased criminal activity in national park units. Experts and media sources linked much of this
illicit activity to urban population growth, increased visitation, and periods
of faltering economic growth.[15]

In addition, crime at LMNRA increased alongside the astonishingly rapid
urban growth of the adjoining area between 1970 and 2000. During this
thirty-year span, the population of Clark County, Nevada, increased from
273,288 to approximately 1.4 million.[16] The overwhelming majority of this
population resided in the metropolitan area of Las Vegas. Correspondingly,
more instances of criminal activity, such as gang violence, vandalism, and
drugs spilled over into the abutting NRA. Between 1989 and 1993, the number of arrests for the possession, distribution, or manufacture of narcotics
increased by 200 and weapons violations from the previous high of twenty
cases to 170. In the year 2000 alone, park rangers responded to 13,537 calls.
They arrested 307 individuals for criminal conduct and nabbed an additional sixty-six fugitives from justice. Such statistics helped rank LMNRA
among the most dangerous units in the national park system by 2000.[17]

Vandalism within park boundaries presented a special problem for
rangers and recreationists. As with other crimes, vandalism spiked as
both the local population and park visitation increased. Between 1989 and
1992, the park reported 65 cases of such acts within LMNRA. By the mid-
1990s reported cases of vandalism surpassed 200 per year. Most often, tar-
gets included visitor and recreational amenities. Park law enforcement
attributed this spike to increased activity within the park by Las Vegas–
based gangs.[18]

One way of keeping a closer eye on illicit activity within the park while
raising much-needed revenue came through building entrance stations
and levying entrance fees. Congress passed legislation in 1997 that allowed
such fees for the first time since the recreation area's creation. Fee collection
began in 2000, after completion of an initial phase of entrance-station construction at automobile access points around the area. At that time, the NPS
implemented a $5 fee per car. Additional fees of $10 for boat launches and
$5 for each additional vessel were also enacted. For frequent users, the NPS
offered annual passes for vehicles and boats at a cost of $20 each. A second
phase of entrance stations was to be completed at a later date.[19]

Locals and the visiting public were skeptical and often outright opposed
to the fees, even as park officials championed the entrance requirement as

FIGURE 4.2. Lake Mead Drive entrance station to the Lake Mead National Recreation Area. Stations were constructed in 2000. Photo: 2010. Photo by author.

a means of raising revenue, improving amenities and visitor experiences, and discouraging illegal activities within the park. Recreationists seemed concerned over whether the fees would actually have such effects. Al Krisch, president of the Lake Mead Boatowners Association, for example, questioned many aspects of fee implementation. Krisch felt that NPS officials had done a poor job of informing the public with specifics regarding applicability, the percentage of money collected that would remain with LMNRA, and how such funds would be used. His organization subsequently initiated a public meeting with NPS officials. In encouraging other organizations and individuals to attend, Krisch warned, "This could be your last chance to speak out!" and that, "As you well know, once a fee is instituted, it seems never to go away."[20] Regardless of Krisch's and others' decision to "speak out" against the fees, access to LMNRA ceased to be free.

In addition to local population growth, urbanization, and regulation of access, LMNRA administrators now found themselves balancing their recreational mission with increased public concern for wildlife preservation. This heightened awareness resulted in increased scrutiny of development and acceptable practices within the NRA's boundaries. Fish, burros, and bighorn sheep became focal points of contention.

Environmentalists began to question the fish-stocking programs that had helped build the NRAs popularity in earlier decades. The issue first presented itself in regard to the Willow Beach National Fish Hatchery. The hatchery was established early in LMNRA's existence to stock the waters below the dam with trout. By the 1990s the facility had placed millions of trout fingerlings in the waters of the Colorado River and nearby Native American reservations.[21]

In 1994, environmentalists charged that rainbow trout populations in Lake Mohave were decimating populations of the endangered bonytail chub and razorback sucker. As a result, the U.S. Fish and Wildlife Service suspended all trout stocking on the lower forty-two miles of Lake Mohave and reduced trout production at Willow Beach by 50 percent. This action produced a significant outcry from local anglers, the Nevada Department of Wildlife, and the superintendent of LMNRA. Fish and Wildlife's failure to inform anyone of this action before suspending stocking on April 12 certainly contributed to the sense of outrage. Within days, petitions by the local Nevada Striper Club and Natural Resources Committee each gained over four thousand signatures opposing the suspension. Likewise, local newspapers lambasted the decision as "haphazard," "irresponsible," "threatening" to local recreation and economic concerns, and hypocritical.[22]

LMNRA officials also had to balance preservation with recreation and safety concerns beyond the reservoirs' banks during this period. Again, the competing interests of various groups and concerns over the environment and safety left the NPS facing difficult conundrums with limited alternatives. NPS actions in response to those alternatives indicated a noticeable shift toward preservationist- and safety-oriented policies over recreational interests throughout the latter decades of the twentieth century.

An example can be found in the NPS's drawn out response to burros. Knowledge of excessive burro populations and the problems they caused in the recreation area had been known since an NPS wildlife study in the late 1930s. Large populations of burros presented a serious problem, as they threatened bighorn sheep and deer populations by depleting already scarce food resources. The study divulged a pressing need to control or even eradicate burros in order to safeguard what it considered the more valuable species. Many nonhunters, though, valued the burros for their historical significance. Later in the twentieth century, animal rights activists and environmentalists also took up the cause of burro protection. Recreation area officials subsequently embarked upon a decades-long search to find an agreeable solution to burro control.[23] Previously instituted methods at other parks offered little in the way of guidance. Public outcry over the NPS policy of shooting burros at Grand Canyon National Park dissuaded officials from adopting a similar extermination plan at LMRNA.[24] Eventually the NPS chose removal over extermination.

In 1948 the park service began issuing permits for the capture of local burros for use as pack animals. The program continued into the 1980s with very limited success, as the burros tended to be extraordinarily difficult to capture. Changing perceptions of wildlife in the 1960s through the 1980s further added to the difficulties of removal or more drastic courses of action, as wildlife protection groups increasingly championed humane treatment and protection of burros.[25]

The 1990s finally brought a solution. A $250,000 increase in funding for resource management, in 1991, allowed officials to place additional emphasis on the burro issue. This resulted in the adoption of a 1995 plan that implemented more humane and effective helicopter roundups of the estimated 1,600 burros within recreation area boundaries. The captured animals were then placed in the Bureau of Land Management's adoption program. By 2000, approximately 90 percent of the burro population had been removed.[26] Although far from perfect—the program still undoubtedly traumatizes the animals and removes them from their wild habitat—it revealed at least a willingness to take environmentalists' concerns into account in making policy decisions.

The management of bighorn sheep presented NPS officials with problems beyond controlling burro populations. Primarily, visitor safety concerns combined with changing attitudes about the perceived right of sportspeople to hunt the sheep on NRA lands and conflicted with established NPS policies.

The NPS had allowed hunting in the LMRNA since the early 1950s.[27] Such a practice was rare within the national park system at that time and speaks to the greater permissiveness with which the NPS managed the recreation area.[28] By the end of the century, limitations were being placed on this permissiveness. Concerns over visitor safety and increasing numbers of recreationists in the area led LMRNA official to restrict the activity." But by the end of the century, such permissiveness had largely ceased. Concerns over visitor safety and increasing numbers of recreationists in the area led LMNRA officials to restrict the activity. Though hunting was still allowed, many areas were declared "no hunting zones," and numerous restrictions and regulations were enforced in areas where the activity remained permissible. In addition to applicable state hunting regulations, hunters at LMNRA were required to abide by the following rules:

1. Loaded weapons may be carried only in hunting zones when actually hunting.
2. Loaded weapons are defined as ANY round in the weapon including the magazine.
3. Target shooting or the discharge of a weapon except to hunt is not permitted.
4. Motorized vehicles may operate on designated public roadways only and must be licensed.[29]

Beyond hunters and wildlife, increased usage and more environmentally aware attitudes of the latter twentieth century also played a role in NPS actions within area boundaries. Specifically, anxiety over pollution and development in the recreation area increased dramatically. Such intrusions, whether in the name of national interest or private profit, have often met strong resistance from environmental organizations, local residents, and the NPS.

Beginning in the early 1970s, for example, the issue of pollution became a rallying point against development at LMNRA. One example was in the fight against the construction of coal-fired power plants in nearby areas beginning in 1971. Proponents of six plants, which were to be built by a consortium of twenty-three electric companies and the U.S. Bureau of Reclamation, argued that the plants were needed to supply additional electricity to the region's burgeoning urban areas. A coalition of environmental groups, consisting of the Black Mesa Defense Fund, Friends of the Earth, the Sierra Club, and Zero Population Growth, charged that the array of power plants would ruin the air over numerous national parks and thirty-nine Native American reservations. A full-page ad taken out by the environmental coalition specifically mentioned LMNRA as endangered by a development that would "spread more deadly smog and soot than currently put out in New York and Los Angeles combined."[30]

Though impassioned, the environmentalists' pleas were largely unheeded. Southern California Edison Company placed the Mohave Generating Station, the second of the six plants, in full operation during 1972. It bordered the Colorado River in the southern tip of Nevada, below Laughlin. Along with the Navajo Generating Station, its predecessor in the Four Corners region, Mohave received a variance from local smog regulations, as neither could meet clean-air standards. In response to concerns over pollution, Edison Vice President Howard P. Allen admitted, "Sure, there is a degradation of air quality in the area," but he downplayed it as merely a matter of aesthetics. This minor impact, he contended, was "worth it" when public demand for electricity was also taken into consideration.[31]

Some twenty years later, another company attempted to build a power plant within LMNRA boundaries. This time, the NPS denied Mead Energy Company permission to carry out an on-site study at the proposed location on the Arizona side of Lake Mead near Gregg's Hideout. The NPS's denial created a great deal of anxiety on the Las Vegas company's part, as it had previously obtained permission from the Federal Energy Regulatory Commission (FERC) and spent approximately $500,000 in preparation. Mead Energy appealed the NPS refusal to Secretary of Interior Bruce Babbitt.[32]

The Department of Interior agreed with its NPS. The Energy Policy Act of 1992 states that the FERC could not issue licenses for electric plants within units of the national park system if the project would adversely affect the local area. The NPS claimed that the Gregg's Hideout plant would have multiple negative effects on the environment, including reduction of wildlife and fish populations, degradation of scenic views, and a limitation of available recreational activities.[33]

A somewhat different environmental objection to development emerged from the Gold Strike Inn's proposed construction of a seventeen-story hotel and casino tower in 1992. Although the Gold Strike Inn was already located within LMNRA boundaries along Highway 93, the most vocal opposition to the tower did not come from the NPS, recreationists, or even environmentalists. Instead, Boulder City residents complained about the development of a major casino and hotel so near their city limits. In a classic example of "not in my backyard" sentiment, several residents complained that they had moved to Boulder City to escape the casinos of Las Vegas. Boulder City was, after all, the only municipality in Nevada where gambling remained illegal. Yet with the construction of the tower, they would find themselves staring directly at a casino from their homes. This, they argued, was not why "they paid a lot of money" to live in the area.[34] They expected the NPS to preserve the aesthetic value of the area.

Even if the NPS did not like the idea of the casino expansion, there was little that could be done about it. The casino had been built some forty years earlier on top of a preexisting and patented "inholding" or private land holding within LMNRA boundaries. As the establishment was privately owned and its thirty-seven acres was zoned for gaming, the NPS had little say in the matter. In fact, the NPS had already attempted to have its say about the casino's existence—and had its hands slapped. Viewing the business as an aberration, NPS officials on numerous occasions sought to purchase and remove it. Such attempts in the 1960s resulted in a 1973 court ruling that prohibited the NPS from further harassing or in any way initiating purchase discussions with casino ownership. As LMNRA Superintendent Alan O'Neill stated in 1992 when asked whether he opposed the casino expansion, "We really can't stop the development. We don't have the authority." [35]

For a brief period during 2003, it seemed as though that authority might again be within reach. That year, casino owners contacted NPS officials to discuss a possible sale. Unfortunately for the NPS and the upset residents of Boulder City, the casino's estimated value had increased dramatically due to its proximity to a proposed Hoover Dam bypass. The proposed bypass promised to increase traffic flow to the casino and, of course, its profitability. Such a newly "lucrative location" prompted Hacienda owners to offer the casino for sale at a price of $30 million. Negotiations soon opened with the NPS, which was willing to offer $20 million for the hotel, casino, and its surrounding acreage. The NPS hoped to demolish the hotel tower and transform the remaining structures into visitor and training centers. Hotel owners finally broke off negotiations in September 2004. They claimed to be concerned about potential job losses for the property's 200 employees and the excessively lengthy transition of occupancy demanded by the NPS. [36]

Hacienda owners finally found an acceptable buyer for the property nine years later. Nevada Restaurant Services, the parent company of Dotty's Casinos, purchased the Hacienda in December 2013. Following an extensive renovation, the new owners rebranded the controversial hotel and casino as the Hoover Dam Lodge in early 2015. The casino remains profitably operational and completely surrounded by NPS managed lands. [37]

Despite its failure to remove the casino, the NPS fared better in relocating residents and mobile homes from dangerous locations in LMNRA during

FIGURE 4.3. The Hacienda Hotel and Casino is located on an inholding within the Lake Mead National Recreation Area. It is visible from the Alan Bible Visitor Center. Photo by author.

these decades. Inhabited zones below the dam had been a source of NPS concern since the 1970s. These areas, particularly around Willow Beach and El Dorado Canyon, had a long history of dangerous flash flooding. In 1974, a flood at El Dorado Canyon killed nine people as it swept away a number of mobile homes. The devastating flood destroyed a marina, a restaurant, a gasoline dock, fifty cars, and twenty mobile homes. Five years later, a U.S. Geological Survey report that had been initiated after the tragic flood listed the trailer park at Willow Beach as also lying in a dangerous flood zone. Upon receiving this report, the NPS ordered closure of the trailer park in July 1979. Residents resisted and pursued legal action, claiming it had been built to U.S. government specifications in 1964. A federal district court judge ruled in favor of the Willow Beach residents in January 1980, allowing the trailer park to remain for the time being.[38]

Yet the issue of flooding and the Willow Beach trailer park was far from settled. In late February 1993, another flash flood caused the temporary evacuation of the trailer park and damages to the Willow Beach and Katherine Landing facilities amounting to $136,000. This flood spurred the NPS to once again order closure of the trailer park. Again, tensions flared between residents and the NPS, culminating in another trip to federal court. This

FIGURE 4.4. Sign warning of flash flood danger in the Willow Creek area of the Lake Mead National Recreation Area, 2010. Courtesy of Marianne Molland.

time, on January 26, 1994, district court judge Robert Broomfield sided with the NPS and ordered residents out and the closure of the trailer park to proceed.[39]

By this time in the mid-1990s, safety concerns had also moved the park service to support removing automobile traffic from the crest of Hoover Dam. Although sufficient to handle traffic flow when it was built in 1936, the two-lane Highway 93 had long been inadequate to accommodate the flow of automobiles between the large urban areas of Phoenix and Las Vegas. Further, the route was determined dangerous, as the winding road to the dam contributed to numerous accidents. The previously mentioned Hoover Dam Bypass project represented an efficient, albeit controversial and expensive, solution to the problem. When completed, the proposed bypass would improve the approach to the dam area and bridge Black Canyon, a short distance downriver from the dam.[40]

On October 31, 1998, the problem seemed well on its way toward a solution as U.S. Senator Harry Reid announced a $4 million federal grant for study and design of the bypass bridge. Within a few months, selection of a bridge site was announced. It was to be located some 1,500 feet downstream from the dam and span Black Canyon at Sugarloaf Mountain with a projected cost of $198 million. It was further reported that, depending on funding, construction should begin in the near future.[41]

Not all, however, were as keen on the idea of this massive undertaking. Opposition to the bridge project appeared almost immediately and from diverse special interest groups. The Sierra Club argued that a better option would be to upgrade the existing route through Laughlin and Bullhead City. This route, it felt, would lessen the environmental impact of the project and locate it outside NPS property. Local Southern Paiutes and Hualapai opposed the bypass because they considered Sugarloaf Mountain a sacred site, which they had historically venerated as a place of healing. Then in November 1999, the discovery of Native American artifacts delayed the project's commencement until an environmental impact study could be completed. Once the study was finished, the government announced, on January 19, 2001, its intention to proceed with the Sugarloaf Mountain site.[42]

At that point, additional and unforeseen objections emerged from the citizens of Boulder City. They complained at town hall meetings that construction of the bypass would likely disrupt the peace of their community by increasing local traffic and were particularly worried about an influx of tractor-trailer traffic. Such traffic, which had avoided the route because of Hoover Dam, could now travel freely. Also, many feared that Congress might designate the bypass as part of the proposed CANAMEX freight route between Canada and Mexico. With the Sierra Club, Boulder City residents proclaimed Laughlin a far better choice for such a project. Approximately 3,000 Boulder City residents signed a petition opposing the route.[43]

As the dam bypass issue remained unsettled and the new century arrived, NPS officials could look back with mixed feelings on sixty-four years of management by LMNRA. Certainly there had been great success in providing recreational opportunities and enjoyment for hundreds of millions of visitors. The area had consistently ranked among the most visited and most popular of all NPS units. In this regard, LMNRA fulfilled its recreational mandate and justified the actions of NPS and USBR officials who, with their 1936 memorandum of agreement, officially acknowledged the need for national recreation areas.

Also, LMNRA's existence certainly can be characterized as a success on the local level. As throngs of recreationists ventured to the park during these decades, they contributed millions upon millions of dollars to the local economy. LMNRA tourism served as an important part of nongaming income for parts of Clark County. Such income was significant by the latter years of the twentieth century. Local businesses, for example, reported about $67 million in nongaming, tourist-related income during the Memorial Day weekend of 1993 alone.[44]

At the same time, it is obvious that in promoting and providing virtually free and unregulated recreational opportunities during its first decades LMNRA was a victim of its own success. Problems associated with overuse, lack of regulation, and shifting social contexts consistently plagued administrators and taxed available resources. The great divergence between recreationists' expectations and NPS abilities and duties was on display as the century drew to a close. Throughout the preceding era, LMNRA and NPS administrators found themselves facing the conundrum of meeting the recreation-first directive while attempting to meet the needs of a rapidly changing and fragmented society. Increased concern over safety, law enforcement, and the environment prompted LMNRA to frequently employ its power of regulation over recreational behavior and accessibility. To an increasing number of recreationists, this seemed a violation of their recreational rights and what they saw as LMNRA's recreation-first mission.

In this regard, the episodes involving visitor safety, implementation of fees, stricter wildlife regulation and protection, attempted removal of non-NPS structures, and the Hoover Dam bypass are significant. Taken together, they indicate a shift in attitude by the NPS and government regarding management of the recreation area. As a whole, these events show a move toward limiting accessibility and more restrictive management of activities within the area. This is a noticeable about-face from the government's earlier emphasis on recreational accessibility and availability. Yet such a shift was largely instigated by the expanding popularity of reservoir-based recreation.

Up against now-entrenched public expectations regarding use of the recreation area—expectations that the historical actions of the NPS itself had created—the park service found itself in a precarious act of balancing perceived recreational rights established in the past with the realities of a greatly altered and much more complex present. The difficulty of this balancing act not only continued into the twenty-first century but intensified as changes in the natural and political landscape, along with the availability of water itself, necessitated even greater restrictions and less access to reservoir-based recreational activities.

NOTES

1. National Park Service, "NPS Stats: Lake Mead NRA," https://irma.nps.gov/Stats/SSRSReports/Park%20Specific%20Reports/Annual%20Park%20Recreation%20Visitation%20%281904%20-%20Last%20Calendar%20Year%29?Park=LAKE (accessed February 22, 2016).

2. Ibid.; National Park Service, "NPS Stats: Ranking Report for Recreation Visits in: 1979–2009," https://irma.nps.gov/Stats/SSRSReports/National%20Reports/Annual%20Park%20Ranking%20Report%20%281979%20-%20Last%20Calendar%20Year%29 (accessed February 22, 2016).

3. "Officers and Youths Clash at Yosemite," *Los Angeles Times,* 5 July 1970; "Youths Battle Park Rangers," *New York Times,* 6 July 1970; Dial Torgerson, "90 Arrested In Yosemite Youth Rampage," *Los Angeles Times,* 6 July 1970.

4. Robert A. Jones, "National Parks: A Report on the Range War at Generation Gap," *New York Times,* 25 July 1971; Charles Wetzel, "Why Blame the Kids," *New York Times,* 15 August 1971.

5. Richard West Sellars, *Preserving Nature in the National Parks* (New Haven: Yale University Press, 1997), 208.

6. Ibid., 208–09; "Park Riot Alert Funds Approved," *Los Angeles Times,* 10 December 1970.

7. John Kimak, "Boating Safety Report Shows Stunning Stats at Lake Mead," *Las Vegas Review-Journal,* 3 August 2000.

8. National Park Service, "Lake Mead NRA," https://irma.nps.gov/Stats/SSRSReports/Park Specific Reports/Annual Park Recreation Visitation (1904 - Last Calendar Year)?Park=LAKE

9. Lupi Saldana, "Safe Boating Week Proclaimed July 4–10," *New York Times,* 24 June 1971.

10. John Kimak, "Wildlife Report Reveals Need for Better Boating Safety," *Las Vegas Review-Journal,* 28 May 1992; John Kimak, "Lake Mead Officials Face Problem of Increase in Crime," *Las Vegas Review-Journal,* 4 March 1993; John Kimak, "Rangers Have Busy Year at Lake Mead," *Las Vegas Review-Journal,* 5 February 1998; Betsy Wade, "Practical Traveler: Staying Safe In the Wild," *New York Times,* 11 April 1999.

11. Keith Rogers, "Lake Mead Fifth in Accidents, Report Says," *Las Vegas Review-Journal,* 6 September 2003.

12. Karen D'Antuono, "The National Park Service's Proposed Ban: A New Approach to Personal Watercraft Use in the National Parks," *Boston College Environmental Affairs Law Review* 27 (2000):243; "Park Service Eyes Rules to Ban Watercraft," *Las Vegas Review Journal,* 20 September 1997; James Splett, "Personal Watercraft Use: A Nationwide Problem Requiring Local Regulation," *Journal of Environmental Law and Regulation* 14 (1999):190–91.

13. "Jet Ski Ban Goes Too Far," *Las Vegas Review-Journal,* 17 July 1998.

14. Marc Reisner and Sarah Bates, *Overtapped Oasis: Reform or Revolution for Western Water* (Washington, D.C.: Island Press, 1990), 35–36.

15. Steve Holland, "Crime Rates in National Parks Soar," *Los Angeles Times,* 4 January 1981.

16. United States Bureau of the Census, Nevada: Population of Counties by Decennial Census, 1900 to 1990, compiled and edited by Richard L. Forstall, Washington, D.C., 1990; United States Bureau of the Census, "Profile of General Demographic Characteristics: 2000," http://factfinder.census.gov/faces/tableservices/jsf/pages /productview.xhtml?src=bkmk (accessed February 10, 2015).

17. John Kimak, "Rangers Have Busy Year at Lake Mead," *Las Vegas Review-Journal,* 5 February 1998; John Kimak, "2000 Statistics Reveal Lake Mead Rangers Kept Busy," *Las Vegas Review-Journal,* 17 June 2001; Gene Mueller, "Shenandoah National Among the Most Dangerous Parks in U.S.," *Washington Times,* 3 September 2003.

18. Ken White, "On Duty at Lake Mead," *Las Vegas Review-Journal,* 21 March 1994; John Kimak, Repair Costs Increasing with Recurring Vandalism at LMNRA," *Las Vegas Review-Journal,* 15 October 1992; John Kimak, "Lake Mead Officials Face Problem of Increase in Crime," *Las Vegas Review-Journal,* 4 March 1993.

19. John Kimak, "Entrance Stations Will End Free Access to Lake Mead," *Las Vegas Review-Journal,* 5 August 1999; Keith Rogers and Natalie Patto, "Fee-Collection Stations Near Completion at Lake Mead," *Las Vegas Review-Journal,* 22 May 2000; Keith Rogers, "Lake Mead Fee Stations Not Ready for Weekend," *Las Vegas Review-Journal,* 1 July 2000.

20. Kimak, "Entrance Stations Will End Free Access to Lake Mead"; Jon Kimak, "Boaters Say Proposed Fees May Be Unfair," *Las Vegas Review-Journal,* 7 October 1999.

21. "The Complete Colorado River," *Los Angeles Times,* 29 November 1970; U.S. Fish and Wildlife Service, "Willow Beach National Fish Hatchery," http://www.fws.gov /SOUTHWEST/fisheries/willow_beach/index.html (accessed February 8, 2016).

22. John Kimak, NDOW Outraged Over Ban on Stocking Trout in Mohave," *Las Vegas Review-Journal,* 28 April 1994; John Kimak, "Trout Dying While FWS Weighs Policy," *Las Vegas Review-Journal,* 16 June 1996; John Kimak, "USFWS Actions Don't Match Words," *Las Vegas Review-Journal,* 28 July 1994.

23. Hal Rothman, "Administrative History of the Lake Mead National Recreation Area," unpublished manuscript in author's possession, 268–69.

24. Ibid., 269–70.

25. Ibid., 272–74; Leon Lindsay, "A Happy Ending to the Saga of Grand Canyon Burros," *Christian Science Monitor,* 10 July 1981, 7.

26. Rothman, "Administrative History," 275–76; "Lake Mead Burros to Be Moved," *Las Vegas Review Journal,* 28 March 1995.

27. Rothman, "Administrative History," 278–80.

28. U.S. Department of Interior, National Park Service, "Lake Mead National Recreation Area: Lake Mead and Lake Mohave," Washington: U.S. Government Printing Office, 1956.

29. National Park Service, "Hunting," http://www.nps.gov/lake/planyourvisit/hunt ingmaps.htm (accessed February 4, 2015).

30. "Like Ripping Apart St. Peters to Sell the Marble," advertisement, *New York Times,* 20 May 1971.

31. Philip Fradkin, "Edison's Nevada Power Plant Generates Ill Will," *Los Angeles Times,* 13 July 1972.

32. Alexander Bloemhof, "Company Lobbies for Chance to Build Lake Mead Plant," *Las Vegas Review-Journal,* 2 May 1993.

33. Ibid.

34. John L. Smith, "Casino Project Near Lake Mead Raises Issue of Sprawl," *Las Vegas Review-Journal,* 31 October 1993.

35. Ibid.; Liz Benton, "Park Service Studying Hacienda Casino Purchase," *Las Vegas Review-Journal,* 28 October 2003.

36. Benton, "Park Service Studying Hacienda Casino Purchase"; Henry Brean, "BLM Wants Casino to Cash Out," *Las Vegas Review-Journal,* 16 February 2004; "Owners end negotiations to sell Hacienda to NPS," *Las Vegas Sun,* 8 September 2004.

37. Steven Slivka, "Boulder City Casino resurrected as Hoover Dam Lodge," *Boulder City Review,* 16 January 2015.

38. "Flood History: Southern Nevada's Worst Floods," *Las Vegas Review-Journal,* 20 August 2003; Earl Gustkey, "Resort Residents Fight Back," *Los Angeles Times,* 12 October 1979; Earl Gustkey, "Willow Beach Fight Not Over," *Los Angeles Times,* 20 June 1980.

39. "Floods Damage Willow Beach," *Las Vegas Review-Journal,* 25 February 1993; "Flood Warning Given To Tenants," *Las Vegas Review-Journal,* 29 June 1993; Keith Rogers, "Willow Beach Dispute Flares," *Las Vegas Review-Journal,* 9 July 1993; John Kimak, "Flood Danger Causing Controversy at Willow Beach," *Las Vegas Review-Journal,* 5 August 1993; John Kimak, "Willow Beach Change Proposed," *Las Vegas Review-Journal,* 4 November 1993; John Kimak, "Services May Cease at Willow Beach," *Las Vegas Review-Journal,* 23 December 1993; Keith Rogers, "Residents Granted Reprieve," *Las Vegas Review-Journal,* 31 December 1993; Keith Rogers, "Willow Beach Tenants Given Notice to Leave," *Las Vegas Review-Journal,* 27 January 1994.

40. Peter O'Connell, "Study: No Bridge Means Woes at Dam," *Las Vegas Review-Journal,* 1 October 1998.

41. Ed Vogel, "Nevada Officials Receive Federal Grant for Hoover Dam Bridge, Other Projects," *Las Vegas Review-Journal,* 31 October 1998; Peter O'Connell, "Feds Choose Route for New Dam Bridge," *Las Vegas Review-Journal,* 9 January 1999.

42. Ibid.; Jan Moller, "Hoover Dam Bypass to be Delayed Further," *Las Vegas Review-Journal,* 9 November 1999; Michael Squires, "Hoover Dam: Agency Selects Bypass Route," *Las Vegas Review-Journal,* 19 January 2001.

43. Michael Squires, "In Regard to Dam Bypass, Boulder City Must Choose Battles Carefully," *Las Vegas Review-Journal,* 22 April 2001; "We're Now A Step Closer to a Police State," *Las Vegas Review-Journal,* 2 May 2001; Michael Squires, "Residents Blast Bypass," *Las Vegas Review-Journal,* 18 April 2001; Trevor Hayes, "Boulder Residents Protest," *Las Vegas Review-Journal,* 23 May 2001.

44. Marcia Pledger, "157,000 Visitors Expected," *Las Vegas Review-Journal,* 28 May 1993.

CHAPTER FIVE

Navigating
the Twenty-First Century

In many regards the trends toward limiting accessibility and increasing reg-ulation in the name of safety and preservation continued into twenty-first century at Lake Mead National Recreation Area. Heavy usage, changing recreational habits, perceptions of criminal and recreational danger, and conflicting demands of various constituencies placed a greater strain on LMNRA administrators. However, drastic environmental changes and polit-ical issues joined with these preexisting problems to make it an even more challenging time. Old problems met new management issues such as how to respond to prolonged drought, the introduction of nonnative species, and the threat of terrorism. The added complexity rendered the successful ful-filment of the recreation-first directive virtually impossible. And restriction of access and regulation of activities conflicted with public expectations of free, safe, and accessible water-based recreation.

In terms of crime in LMNRA, the 2000s were little different from the 1990s. Spillover from metropolitan Las Vegas of urban gang issues, drug-and alcohol-related crime, and vandalism continued to require much effort and expenditure. As LMNRA Chief Ranger Dale Antonich told ABC News in 2003, "Just about any type of crime that goes on in any urban environment happens out here."[1] The same year, the *Los Angeles Times* reported that rang-ers classified LMNRA as fifth among the ten most dangerous NPS units. This ranking was attributed to gang activity, extraordinarily heavy usage of the lake, and insufficient law-enforcement personnel to patrol the area's vast expanse.

The lack of officers was particularly challenging. The year 2003 saw a force of only thirty-six rangers attempting to safeguard almost eight million visitors in an area the size of Delaware.[2] Perhaps it was some consolation that LMNRA rangers, as limited as they were in number, had use of the only military-style armored vehicle owned by any NPS unit.[3] Then again, that the perceived need for such a vehicle existed on NPS-managed grounds was disheartening.

Rangers often blamed the continuing shortage of law-enforcement personnel on insufficient budgets and a bureaucratic culture among park administrators that seemed abnormally resistant to change. Other proponents of increased law enforcement in the parks, such as U.S. Senator Charles Grassley (R-IA), argued that the Department of Interior and NPS officials had an interest in downplaying the impact of crime within NPS units in order to maintain the system's wholesome image. This, in turn, contributed to insufficient funds, lack of training, and, in the end, diminished visitor safety and experience. Randall Kendrick, the executive director of the U.S. Park Rangers Lodge of the Fraternal Order of Police, called for a significant increase in the number of rangers and for the management of law enforcement to be taken from park superintendents.[4]

Organ Pipe National Park Superintendent Bill Wellman, on the other hand, opposed the push for increased law enforcement activity in the parks. He asserted that Kendrick's and similar ideas were not suited for the NPS. Rangers were responsible for much more than law enforcement and were often the human faces of the parks. As such, Wellman argued that public expectations would not allow for more active and numerous rangers. Quite simply, he believed that the visiting public did not want to see "rangers with the same hard edge as FBI agents." Instead, the public expected "park rangers to be cut from the same cloth as a Boy Scout."[5]

While additional funding for law enforcement for the NPS was certainly needed by the early twenty-first century, the perception of NPS units as dangerous and violent places must be questioned. In 2006, eleven deaths were investigated throughout the entire national park system. That year, the park system hosted some 273 million visitors. Even though one of these deaths occurred at LMNRA, it was eventually ruled a suicide.[6] This is an investigated death rate of about .004 per 100,000 visitors for the park system as a whole, and .01 per 100,000 visitors for LMNRA. Meanwhile, neighboring Las Vegas experienced 152 murders in 2006, for a murder rate of 11.6 per 100,000 inhabitants.[7] Nonetheless, the perception of violently dangerous national parks took root in the press, and, when politically expedient, in the halls of government. This process was very similar to what took place in previous decades regarding the perception of high rates of accidental death in LMNRA.

The political value of extolling the "danger" of the parks is rooted in a public expectation of nearly safe and worry-free experiences within NPS units. Certainly, historical NPS actions in the national parks from the Mather era through the conclusion of Mission 66 have contributed to the development of such unreal expectations. Since its earliest times, the NPS has had a history of manipulating the national park environments to provide safe and enjoyable tourist experiences. Such manipulations have included road building and flora control to "frame" views to achieve the most aesthetically pleasing effect and predator control for visitor safety and to protect more popular wildlife species. In reality, the pristine but safe "wilderness" that recreationists viewed from their car windows was not as untouched and, without NPS intervention, certainly not as safe as it seemed. Much of what the public believed to be "natural" within the parks was a cultural construct built by NPS manipulations founded on viewing the "wild" from the safety of paved roads and four-wheeled, fossil-fuel-powered cocoons.[8]

Further, American society in the early twenty-first century has grown hypersensitive and intent on protecting itself from danger, difficulty, and struggle. This is an age when university administrators discipline professors for challenging students' worldviews and making them uncomfortable. In class, the same professors are expected to issue "micro-aggression" warnings before uttering any phrases that might induce their students to recall traumatic experiences or otherwise feel uncomfortable. Heaven forbid that a historian should discuss "violation" of treaties or "conquest" of regions without forewarning to allow students to evacuate the lecture hall. In this context, we cannot be surprised that people expect safety and accessibility and are susceptible to tales of danger, even on very safe NPS lands.[9]

Nonetheless, some forms of crime certainly marred many recreationists' visits to LMNRA during the early 2000s. Property crimes were particularly difficult to control and had a distinctly negative effect on visitor experience. Vandalism and graffiti, for example, ruined scenery and damaged cultural resources. One shocking instance of criminal vandalism occurred in 2010 when individuals splattered petroglyphs at Grapevine Canyon with paint using paintball guns. Such actions resulted in expensive cleanup (when possible) and the closing of some sites to visitors.[10]

While visitor experience was more affected by property crime than violence, accidents also remained a source of concern. Throughout this period, LMNRA continued to rank among the top of all NPS units in number of visitor accidents. This should not be surprising, given its annual use by millions of water-oriented recreationists. While accidental death rates among visitors remained low, other forms of accidents were more common. In the year 2001, for example, park officials documented 183 boating accidents and 145 automobile-related accidents.[11] The accident rate is thus approximately 3.9 per 100,000 visitors for 2001.[12] Although the number seems relatively low, it is important to remember that the calculation includes all recreational visitors. If it were possible to calculate a rate relative to the number of visitors who participated in boating or driving, the rate per 100,000 would undoubtedly increase. Thus, recreational safety remained a primary concern and required ever-increasing expenditures through the early 2000s. In an acknowledgment of how seriously administrators took the issue, LMNRA Strategic Plan for 2001–2005 listed improved safety and the reduction of accidents as primary goals for the five-year period.[13]

Safety concerns also prompted park officials to embrace modern communications technology by constructing four cell-phone towers. One incident illustrating the value of such coverage occurred in 2003. That year, two families were marooned on Boulder Island after experiencing boat problems. Their attempts to contact authorities by radio failed. The boaters were rescued only after a passing boater discovered their predicament and used his cell phone to contact authorities.[14]

Yet despite the increased expenditures and emphasis on safety, water-associated accidents continued to be a problem. Ten people, for example, died from drowning and boating-related accidents in the year 2005 alone. A variety of factors contributed to the incidents and resultant deaths. These included alcohol consumption while operating watercraft and automobiles, lack of boat training, receding water levels exposing previously submerged obstructions, and the popularity of new, more dangerous forms of water recreation. The latter source of accidents included the growing popularity of personal watercraft (PWC) and at one point such dangerous innovations as flying rafts, inflatables designed to become airborne when towed at high speeds behind motorboats. Within four months of the rafts' introduction on Lake Powell, four recreationists received injuries severe enough to require airlift. Injuries related to the devices at Lake Mead led park officials to ban them.[15]

In regulating personal watercraft, LMNRA faced much greater opposition than when it banned the flying rafts. PWCs were far more popular, and any proposed regulation proved to be very contentious. As discussed in chapter 4, many groups, ranging from anglers to swimmers to environmental activists, favored strict regulation or outright ban of the devices, which the NPS did consider in the late 1990s. Environmental groups sued for greater PWC regulation on NPS-managed waters. One such lawsuit, brought by Bluewater Network, resulted in a September 15, 2002, court-imposed deadline for NRAs to have PWC plans in place. As this deadline approached, the NPS had not approved the various NRAs' PWC studies. LMNRA's study, which had been completed for some time, recommended the continued PWC usage on the area's reservoirs, albeit more restricted. Yet due to the inaction of the NPS, rumors developed among pro-PWC recreationists. Soon, many were asserting that all NRAs would be closed when the deadline passed without implementation of a PWC plan. In response, the American Watercraft Association and pro-PWC recreationists organized a protest on Lake Mead on September 14, 2002, dramatically billed as a "last ride" on the lake before its closure.[16]

In reality, the court order required only that all PWC use on the lakes be temporarily halted if the NPS did not have plans in place by the September deadline. In early September, the NPS reached an agreement with Bluewater Network to extend the deadline into early 2003. Still, even the threat of recreation area closure or PWC ban prompted direct action among recreationists, who were "outraged" at this attempt to regulate their "family recreation."[17]

In accordance with the revised agreement with Bluewater Network, the NPS released its final management plan regarding PWC usage on Lake Mead and Lake Mohave in spring 2003. First, the plan stated that all two-stroke PWC engines must be replaced by less polluting four-stroke engines by 2013. Of more immediate concern, the plan allowed for the continuation of PWC activity on 95 percent of LMNRA's waterways, with the remaining 5 percent designated primitive or semiprimitive. The NPS applied the semiprimitive and primitive designations to the section of Black Canyon from Willow Beach to Hoover Dam, Bonelli Bay, and the Lake Mead confluence with the Muddy River. In addition, the final rule expanded no-wake zones around bathing beaches from 100 to 200 feet from the shoreline.[18] This compromise solution attempted to balance the recreational needs and expectations of all involved interest groups.

One area in which area administrators did not compromise was with entrance fees. The controversial fee program exhibited great potential early on. Over the course of a five-day period ending with Memorial Day 2001—the first major holiday for which the fee stations were open—the park collected some $165,409. Regulations concerning the fees required that 80 percent of all money collected remain within the recreation area. LMNRA was in great need of such additional funds, as by 2001 it had a $187 million backlog for maintenance and new construction. The remaining 20 percent of fees went toward smaller parks, national monuments, and historical sites within the NPS system that did not charge entrance fees.[19]

Yet, in the context of increasing costs and decreasing federal funding, the entrance fees still proved wildly insufficient to meet park needs. In 2011, continuing revenue shortfalls forced an increase in entrance fees at LMNRA. Beginning on January 15 of that year, fees increased from $5 to $10 per car for five-day access. Likewise, annual passes increased from $20 to $30, and watercraft fees increased from $10 for a five-day pass to $16 for a seven-day pass. The rationale was founded on revenue shortfalls due to the severe economic downturn of recent years, plus the expenses incurred as the park attempted to deal with prolonged drought conditions. By then, the NPS had spent approximately $36 million within the recreation area to deal with declining water levels. Park officials estimated that the increased fees would help the area's gross revenue increase from $3.3 million in 2010 to approximately $13 million by 2014.[20]

Regardless of any economic necessity for the fees, groups such as the Lake Mead Boat Owners Association objected to changes in the fee structure. President Wen Baldwin cautioned that further increases would result in lower recreation area visitation and accessibility.[21] Others, such as Kingman, Arizona, journalist Don Martin argued that the fee increases were unnecessary. The basis for his conclusion was that many LMNRA visitors did not use the fee-free NPS units that received the other 20 percent of LMNRA fee revenue. Why, he asked, "should we pay for other national park sites that currently don't charge a recreation fee?" He proposed that visitors to those sites should "pay an equal and fair share."[22]

Despite such opposition, park fees continued to rise with mounting operational costs. By early 2015, LMNRA was planning another fee hike. This proposed increase was significant, doubling existing fees in many cases. Individual entry fees were to increase from $5 to $10 per person, automobile fees from $10 to $20 per car, and camping fees from $10 to $20 per night. Annual entrance fees would increase as well from $30 to $40 per year, and annual watercraft fees would increase from $30 to $50 per year.[23]

As with the previous fee increases, recreationists objected to the additional expense and loss of accessibility. People posting comments on BigFish.com's popular Nevada Fishing Forum's message board uniformly opposed the rate increases. One angler, posting under screen name Wolfs4evr, characterized the fee increase as "insane." Another, under the screen name Mojave Red, objected to the rate increase on the basis of reduced access and the perceived misuse of previously collected fees. Mohave Red expressed a wish to see "something positive coming from my money and not just more areas you cone-off not allowing access to." Others, such as a poster with the screen name iamthesmf, echoed concerns heard in 2010. To iamthsmf, the fees were possibly unfair, as nothing ensured that "money collected at Lake Mead stays at Mead."[24]

Although some of the complaints of iamthsmf and others might have been warranted, neither the NPS nor LMNRA had any control over one major cause of increased expenditures during this period. A significant amount of the money raised by the entrance and usage fees since their implementation went to facility upgrades necessitated by declining water levels. As waters diminished, LMNRA shouldered significant expenses to extend boat ramps, move marinas, and protect newly exposed cultural resources. By 2015, LMNRA officials estimated that drought-related expenditures would amount to $5 million over the next two years just for ramp extensions, replacing navigation buoys, and moving amenities such as bathrooms.[25]

By that time, the drought was in its sixteenth year. Beginning in 1999, the Colorado River basin entered the driest period of its recorded history. As snowfalls throughout the watershed decreased, the yearly runoff that fed the reservoir declined dramatically. Water levels in Lake Mead fell rapidly to a point not seen since the reservoir's creation. The extent of the declining water levels drastically affected recreational activities, accessibility, and the operation of facilities at LMNRA.[26]

By mid-October 2010, the then eleven-year-old drought had lowered water at Lake Mead to 1937 levels. On the morning of October 18, water surface was at an elevation of 1,083 feet, a full 146 feet from full-pool level of 1,229 feet, and less than 40 percent of the reservoir's capacity. Officials were now publicly expressing concerns about disruption of services should the drought continue. Speaking on Las Vegas's local CBS news affiliate months earlier, Southern Nevada Water Authority (SNWA) head Pat Mulroy painted a grim picture: "When we hit 1,025 (feet), we will have stopped generating

FIGURE 5.1. "Bathtub ring" reveals the declining water level of Lake Mead, 2010. Courtesy of Marianne Molland.

electricity. When we hit 1,025, the amount of water left in Lake Mead is barely enough to meet a single year's allocation." Other officials, such as USBR Lower Colorado Regional Director Lori Gray-Lee, admitted that there was a 20 percent chance of the water level falling below the crucial 1,025-foot level within two years. In addition to interrupting electricity output, this would lead to water shortages in the Las Vegas Valley. Over the last three decades, the rapidly expanding urban area had grown to depend upon the lake for 90 percent of its drinking water.[27]

Low water levels at Lake Mead were significantly affecting recreational activities at LMNRA by April 2010. As the water receded, traditional entry points for boating and other water sports were left literally high and dry. At Overton Beach, falling water levels resulted in the closure of the lake's northernmost access point for anglers and boaters. Likewise, the popular site offered one of the lake's most impressive marinas, camping facilities, a store, dining, and a long-term trailer park. These facilities were ill equipped to survive a decade-long drought.[28]

The demise of Overton Beach began in early 2007, as low water necessitated moving marina facilities to other locations. Without the marina

FIGURE 5.2. The boat launch at Las Vegas Bay Marina was far from Lake Mead's water by 2010. Photo by author.

nearby, and the beach's boat launch sitting on dry land, the RV park, store, gas station, boat-storage area, and maintenance areas closed on March 31. By 2010, cattle navigated the buoys that once guided boaters into the marina, and the old boat launch itself could be seen a half-mile from the new shoreline. The NPS cut off access completely to Overton Beach on April 25 of that year, when it closed the access road.[29]

The relocation and closing of Overton Beach was not an isolated consequence of the drought. Low water levels required the relocation of marinas and disruption of recreational services all over the recreation area. As early as 2001, NPS officials closed the boat launch at Pearce Ferry due to low water and silt buildup. By early 2004, popular launch ramps at Hemenway Harbor and Callville Bay likewise faced possible closure. By this time, three of the lake's ten public launches were closed. Almost three years earlier, receding water had forced the relocation of Las Vegas Marina from Las Vegas Bay to Horsepower Cove in Hemenway Harbor. Since then, falling water levels have forced the marina to follow the receding lakeshore on six occasions. Each move cost between $25,000 and $50,000.[30]

As the drought continued, costs and impact on recreation mounted. Callville Bay's boat ramp, for example, managed to remain open only by continual extension to keep pace with the waterline. Boaters faced bottleneck

FIGURE 5.3. Sign announcing the closure of boat-launch facilities at Lake Mead's Government Wash due to low water conditions, 2010. Courtesy of Marianne Molland.

delays at remaining boat ramps by 2007. By early 2008, water levels also forced the reconfiguration of Echo Bay Marina. It closed for approximately one week in early March, as workers relocated the marina some 160 feet farther out.[31]

Beyond inconveniencing boaters, the constant race between marina facilities and the retreating water line was enormously expensive. Calculations indicated that for every twenty-foot drop in the lake level, the NPS was forced to spend approximately $5 million on facility relocation and extension. LMNRA park planner John Holland estimated that the NPS incurred about $4 million in drought-related expenses on Boulder Harbor, Callville Bay, Temple Bar, and South Cove in the spring and summer of 2007 alone.[32]

Non-NRA expenditures also mounted, due to the dependence of metropolitan Las Vegas upon the reservoir for its water supply. Since 1971, the Las Vegas Valley Water District (LVWD) has drawn its water from Lake Mead to supplement insufficient groundwater. By 2010, the lake accounted for approximately 90 percent of Las Vegas's drinking water. Between 1971 and 2004, the water district siphoned this water through two intake pipes at Saddle Island. As water levels declined, the water drawn through increasingly shallower intakes grew warmer. This resulted in higher concentrations of pollutants. As a remedy, the Southern Nevada Water Authority (SNWA)

FIGURE 5.4. Floating structures at Callville Bay Marina, 2010. Photo by author.

spent $6.4 million on a 140-foot extension of one of the two intake pipes. The extension placed the intake in the old Colorado River channel, where the coolest and purest water was found.[33]

By spring 2008, the omnipresent drought forced SNWA to take on even more expensive and drastic measures. This took the form of a third intake that would allow the continued drawing of water, even if falling levels forced the closure of the two "straws" already in existence. This intake, initially slated for completion in 2013, would consist of a three-mile-long tunnel underneath the lake's floor designed to connect to a large, concrete intake funnel resembling a bathtub drain on the lake's bottom. Obviously a daunting task, tunnel construction faced numerous delays in the following years. In July 2010, workers for the project's general contractor, Vegas Tunnel Constructors, encountered an unstable fault zone in a cavern at about 600 feet. The tunnel then flooded with a mucky mixture of water and clay. This necessitated the sealing and forced filling of the cavern with grout, which in turn threw the tunnel's construction many months behind schedule. In December, the project flooded again. Thus, as 2010 drew to an end, the tunnel project sat stymied as engineers attempted to devise a solution for the area's unstable geology. Reportedly, each day spent idle added an

FIGURE 5.5. Water intake "straws" at Saddle Island, Lake Mead National Recreation Area, 2010. Photo by author.

additional $30,000 to the project's overall cost.[34] The tunnel finally reached its destination in late 2014.[35]

Almost a year later, on September 23, 2015, and with the reservoir at a mere 38 percent capacity, workers removed the 8.6-ton iron ball that capped the deepwater intake. Two years behind schedule and at a final cost of $817 million, the third intake went into operation. Engineers and the press compared the construction of the intake to that of the Lincoln Tunnel and even the Hoover Dam itself. Interestingly, the dam cost $49 million to construct when completed in 1936, equivalent to approximately $840 million in today's money.[36] Regardless of such cost similarities, the reservoir's waters could now be drawn down to the last drop if urban need and southwestern drought so required.

In addition to limiting access and initiating such expensive and difficult construction projects, receding water levels changed the nature of recreational activities in the area. On one hand, the low water presented more dangerous conditions for boaters. Underwater obstructions, safely submerged for years, projected from the water or, worse yet, lurked just below the water's surface. Further, warning buoys placed at times of full pool drifted in excess of 100 feet from their original locations. Even bathers faced increased risk, as the drying beach areas and adjacent shallow water exposed broken glass and other refuse.[37]

But with the new dangers, low water levels offered up objects of a more culturally valuable sort, as formerly submerged cultural resources began resurfacing. The town of St. Thomas, for example, reappeared in 2002. Two years later, historical sites linked to the construction of Hoover Dam also emerged, including a concrete water tank and pump house used during dam construction. These sites reappeared for the first time since the mid-1960s drawdown that accompanied the filling of Lake Powell.[38]

The emergence of these objects created additional expense and effort for the NPS, as well as tension with locals concerning recreation area usage. Faced with looting at the historical sites—arrests were made—the NPS found itself forced to prepare a Submerged Cultural Resource Management Plan. News of this undertaking and the NPS's desire to protect the sites sparked some degree of public dissatisfaction. A *Las Vegas Review-Journal* editorial called efforts to protect these resources "a bunch of bunk" and "an absurd abuse of federal power." In the editor's opinion, such protection impeded the area's proper and officially designated duty as a recreation area. "Relic hunting" represented an acceptable form of recreation.[39]

The drought also played a large role in national media coverage of LMNRA. Regularly, the white "bathtub ring" around Lake Mead was equated with endangered water and electricity supplies for urban areas. In a way, this associated LMNRA with the idea of overdevelopment of the arid West. As articles stressed the reevaluation and serious steps that would be necessary if the water level continued to fall, they reinforced the idea of a region living beyond its resource capacity. As a 2015 *New York Times* article related, any adjustment to water usage agreements regarding the reservoir is just a "stopgap solution that is unlikely to solve the problems of a region whose demand for water far exceeds what the Colorado is able to deliver."[40]

Other articles in the national media also equated the diminishing waters of Lake Mead with the prospective demise of a region living beyond its means. In January of 2011, for example, *The Economist* ran a story highlighting the drought, its impact on Lake Mead, and the threat to the wider West. Specifically, the article referred to the "crisis" of "civilization" in the region, brought about by its dependence upon reservoirs and changing environmental characteristics. In a stereotypical reference to Las Vegas and its precarious position of depending upon Lake Mead for 90 percent of its water supply, the article related how "Sin City" is "a canary in the mine shaft" when

TABLE 5.1. Lake Mead National Recreation Area annual visitation, 1990–2014.

Year	Recreational Visitation	Year	Recreational Visitation
1990	8,582,223	2003	7,915,581
1991	8,445,016	2004	7,819,984
1992	9,016,525	2005	7,692,438
1993	8,941,225	2006	7,777,753
1994	9,566,725	2007	7,622,139
1995	9,838,702	2008	7,601,863
1996	9,350,847	2009	7,668,689
1997	8,528,420	2010	7,080,758
1998	8,788,055	2011	6,396,682
1999	9,023,943	2012	6,285,439
2000	8,755,005	2013	6,344,714
2001	8,465,547	2014	6,942,873
2002	7,550,284		

Note: Of the eight National Recreation Areas based on U.S. Bureau of Reclamation–developed reservoirs and managed by the National Park Service, only Lake Mead and Lake Meredith (TX) exhibited the pattern of visitation shown by these numbers over the course of the early twenty-first century. (National Park Service, "Annual Recreation Visitation Report by Years: 2004 to 2014," https://irma.nps.gov/Stats/SSRSReports/System Wide Reports/Annual Recreation Visitation By Park (1979 - Last Calendar Year)?RptYear=2014. Table by author.)

considering the region's possible demise.[41] Another article in *USA Today* directly linked the lake's current image with the drought and western aridity. Characterizing the Colorado River as "the most over-allocated in the world," the writer described Lake Mead as a "very visual if not frightening reminder of the severity of the drought."[42]

One has to wonder whether such media scrutiny of the lake relative to the drought and perceived overdevelopment of the Southwest influenced, in any way, the decrease in recreational visitation numbers during the corresponding period. LMNRA visitation rates generally increased from the park's creation through the 1990s, peaking during that decade with visitation surpassing nine million in 1992, 1994, 1995, 1996, and 1999. A significant downward trend in visitation began in 2000. From 2000 to 2001, visitation rates dropped into the eight million range and remained in the seven million range during the next eight years. Beginning in 2011, visitation dipped into the six million range and remained there through 2014 (Table 5.1).[43] While contextual events during this period, such as the terrorist attacks of September 11, 2001, the Great Recession of 2008, and the rise of other forms of recreation related to the Internet and gaming likely influenced visitation as well, it seems likely that increased knowledge of declining environmental conditions also played a role. It should also be noted that decreasing visitation also coincided with the NPS's decision to enact entrance and user fees at the recreation area.

In addition to shaping perceptions of the reservoir relative to southwestern resource capacity and perhaps influencing visitation, the prolonged drought likewise affected wildlife management issues during the 2000s. And this influenced recreation directly. Specifically, the Lake Mead Fish Hatchery succumbed to decreasing water levels in 2007. The fishery had long depended upon the Basic Magnesium Industries' (BMI) pipeline for water. The 14-mile pipeline, constructed during World War II to provide BMI with water for magnesium ingot production, was ill suited for fishery supply purposes in the 2000s. As water levels receded, the intake pipe became ever closer to the surface. At its original depth of 130 feet, the pipe drew in cold water. But as the water depth dropped, due to drought and overallocation, it began to take in warmer water. The warmer water presented an insurmountable problem, as rainbow trout rearing requires cold-water temperatures.[44]

While the hatchery shutdown resulted in fewer gamefish for Lake Mead anglers, its closure wasn't just because of the warming water. Another far more devastating wildlife issue also appeared in the first decade of the twenty-first century. This episode began on January 6, 2007 as a Las Vegas Boat Harbor employee discovered a small mussel attached to a breakwater anchor cable. The discovery of what appeared to be a zebra mussel set off a flurry of activity over the next few years at the reservoir. Much effort and money was subsequently thrown at controlling the invaders' impact on Lake Mead and potential spread to other southwestern waters.[45]

Upon close examination, experts determined that the mystery mollusks were an even greater problem than first suspected, for they turned out to be quagga mussels. The quagga mussel belongs to the same genus as the zebra mussel yet is larger and far more prolific. Wildlife experts have referred to it as a zebra mussel on steroids. Its discovery in Lake Mead marked the first instance of the species west of the Mississippi River.[46]

The mussels were, in fact, a nonnative species in North America. Quagga and zebra mussels originated in Ukraine and first appeared in the Great Lakes region during the late 1980s. Most experts believe they were introduced via the ballast tanks of European-origin commercial ships. Once established in the Great Lakes, the mussels were damaging, expensive, and incredibly prolific. Unchecked by natural predators, they quickly infested many waterways of the eastern U.S. and parts of Canada. Where present, they reproduced extraordinarily rapidly and obtained mind-boggling densities. In some places, populations surpassed 700,000 mussels per square meter.[47]

Such high densities caused extensive property and environmental damage. The mussels clogged pipes, blocked water inlets, littered beaches with sharp shells, and coated the bottoms of boats. Environmentally, their unchecked presence was equally devastating. The mussels' rapid consumption of planktonic algae upset the food chain and contributed to the growth of dangerous cyanobacteria, whose large-scale blooms frequently resulted in aquatic dead zones. Further, the mussels' feeding and defecating characteristics introduced increased levels of heavy metals and PCBs into the food chain, for they filtered heavy metals and PCBs from the water. In this regard, the mussels' presence might be viewed as advantageous to polluted waterways. Unfortunately, the dangerous elements do not remain within the mussels but are released in concentrated form as highly toxic pellets. Bottom-feeding species then eat the pellets and are, in turn, consumed by other predators. The toxins thus travel from the mussel all the way to humans. Along each step of the food chain, the toxin level accumulates through a process known as biomagnification.[48]

Fully aware of the consequences of zebra and quagga mussel introduction, LMNRA officials had been taking measures to keep them out for years. Rangers had long checked for mussels on many out-of-state vessels. In one 2004 episode, a diligent ranger—Marc Burt—spotted zebra mussels on a houseboat from Kentucky attempting to launch at Temple Bar. The boat was impounded, cleaned, and quarantined for a month. Unfortunately, given that mussel larvae are microscopic and can be present in foreign water transported within a boat, and that LMNRA's ranger force has been consistently understaffed, a 100 percent detection rate was impossible. At some point between 2004 and 2007, quagga mussels were introduced into the waters of Lake Mead.[49]

Anxious officials first declared (and hoped) that the infestation was limited to the area where the first mussels had been discovered. Further examination revealed a different story. Within days, Lake Mead Boat

Owners Association President and mussel monitoring program volunteer, Wen Baldwin found numerous mussels at Lake Mead Marina. By January 23, 2007 divers and searchers had confirmed populations at Callville Bay, Kingman Wash, Katherine Landing, in a California aqueduct reservoir, and in the Southern Nevada Water Authority and BMI water intakes at Saddle Island. The BMI pipe supplied water to Henderson, Lake Las Vegas, numerous industries along Lake Mead Parkway, and, as mentioned, the Lake Mead Fish Hatchery. The mussels were found to have colonized the hatchery as well, and that infestation, along with low water levels, spelled its closure.[50]

With the mussel invasion at an alarming and rapidly increasing level, the federal government took action. By late January, 2007, Department of the Interior officials had created a multistate effort aimed at containing the mollusks' spread from Lake Mead and Lake Mohave. In early March, the Environmental Protection Agency (EPA) called for interagency cooperation in controlling the quaggas. During hearings before the House of Representatives' Water Resources and Environment Subcommittee, EPA Assistant Administrator Benjamin Grumbles proposed that rapid-response protocols be adopted and that the Army Corps of Engineers, Coast Guard, and Departments of Interior, Agriculture, and Commerce all join the fight. Representative Jon Porter (R-NV) likewise sponsored a bill granting the NPS greater authority to take action against the quagga mussels, even if such actions had ramifications in areas beyond national park boundaries. The bill passed by a vote of 390 to 10 and marked a significant departure from policies that had historically allowed the NPS to spend budget appropriations only on programs within park borders.[51]

Despite such actions, the mussels continued to spread and reproduce. With no effective means of control and no local predators, mussel populations blossomed in Lake Mead and Lake Mohave. By July 2009, the population in the two lakes had soared into the trillions. Hoover Dam's intake towers now had mussel colonies with densities of 55,000 per square foot. Mussels also were showing up in coolant pipes for the power plant's generators and other intake structures. Wildlife officials found eradication impossible. Warm water, high calcium content in the water, the female quagga mussels' ability to release a million eggs per year, and the inability to filter out microscopic quagga larvae rendered futile all attempts to control populations on the lakes. To make matters worse, the mussels reproduced in Lake Mead at a rate three times faster than they had in the Great Lakes.[52]

FIGURE 5.6. Mussel awareness signs reveal concern over the spread of invasive quagga mussels, 2010. Courtesy of Marianne Molland.

By this time, state and federal agencies were spending "untold millions" in efforts to contain the mussels in the Colorado River reservoirs. Programs enacted ranged from the NPS's "Don't Move a Mussel" informational campaign to quarantining boats from infected waterways and mandatory decontamination. At Lake Mead, boats had to undergo decontamination *before* removal. Prior to launching on Lake Powell, upstream of Lake Mead, regulations required inspection of all craft. California placed specially trained mussel-sniffing dogs at inspection points. If the dogs indicated the presence of mussels on a watercraft, it was impounded and quarantined.[53]

Such activities, along with the increasing numbers of mussels, created problems for boat owners and recreationists on Lake Mead and Lake Mohave. In addition to the aggravation and delays inherent with inspections and decontaminations, boat owners faced the expensive task of having their crafts' hulls cleansed of mussels several times a year. Failure to remove the mussels affected boat operation through weight and drag. Further, concentrations of mussels clogged engine-water intakes, which in turn led to overheating and failure. Cleaning and preventive maintenance could cost thousands of dollars per year, depending on boat size.[54]

Faced with such expense, boat owners looked to the NPS. Many called for the creation of NPS-constructed facilities within LMNRA for the removal of mussels from boat hulls. Recreation area officials countered that any technology used for mussel removal would be exceedingly difficult and expensive, as it would have to meet environmental standards of both Arizona and Nevada. Likewise, LMNRA spokesperson Roxanne Dey asserted that researching safe mussel removal practices should not be the taxpayers' responsibility. Boat owners, she said, should "do [their] own homework" regarding environmentally acceptable and safe methods. The NPS, she went on, could not allow chemicals, divers, and other equipment around busy marinas because of safety and environmental concerns. Thus, the NPS refused to consider the boat owners' proposal. And, she informed upset boaters, the NPS was "not going to do one thing that gets rid of quaggas on the hull that creates another problem environmentally."[55]

As in earlier decades, the challenges that administrators faced in wildlife management did not end at the shoreline. Land-based wildlife concerns joined with the mussel infestation to present impossibly difficult management challenges. One particularly divisive issue involved predator control during the 2000s. Specifically, a plan to kill ten or more mountain lions within the recreation area's boundaries drew protests from environmentalists. The Arizona Department of Game and Fish conceived the culling plan in an attempt to protect bighorn sheep populations on the Arizona side of the river. A great deal of criticism was directed at the NPS for allowing Arizona Game and Fish to develop the plan. Frank Bouno, a longtime NPS employee and board member of the group Public Employees for Environmental Responsibility, said that any such action should be a "last resort" and called for more public discussion and environmental assessment. Ecologist Daniel Patterson of the Center for Biological Diversity condemned the plan as a mistake. Emphasizing the scarcity of mountain lions, he argued that ecosystem-level management was needed rather than single-species management.[56]

Finally, and largely unrelated to wildlife, traffic management and wider political issues continued to plague NPS and LMNRA officials throughout the early 2000s. The issue of the Hoover Dam Bypass, specifically, assumed greater importance for the NPS following the terrorist attacks of September 11, 2001. With the dam listed as a prospective target and truck traffic across it banned, a security-based push to remove all through-traffic from the top of the dam quickly overwhelmed local opposition to the bypass route. In the months following the attacks, state and federal officials urged that the project be fast-tracked.[57]

With preliminary engineering studies completed by June 2002, work on the dam bypass began on October 21. Scheduled for completion in 2007, the bypass and bridge was championed by Governor Kenny Guinn (R), Representative Jim Gibbons (R-NV), Nevada Department of Transportation Director Tom Stephens, and Chairman of the U.S. House of Representatives Committee on Transportation and Infrastructure Don Young (R-AK) as key to reducing terrorist threats to Hoover Dam and Lake Mead, securing Nevada's place on the CANAMEX route, and improving transportation flow and safety between Las Vegas and Phoenix. At this time, the cost estimate for the bypass and 1,900-foot bridge was pegged between $231 and $234 million.[58]

Despite the fast tracking of the project, the process was neither quick nor smooth, and actual construction did not begin until 2005. Obayashi Corporation and PSM Construction USA partnered to win the bridge contract with a low bid of $114 million. The partnership did not experience the same level of success in this massive enterprise as Six Companies, Inc. had some seventy years earlier with Hoover Dam.[59]

The main obstacle faced by construction partnership, other than the 1,900-foot span and 890-foot depth of Black Canyon, was wind. High winds repeatedly delayed construction efforts early on. On September 15, 2006, the twin 280-foot crane towers sustaining the high-line system required for the bridge's construction collapsed. This collapse caused a one-year delay, while the crane system was redesigned and replaced. In addition to throwing the project behind schedule, the disaster helped push costs over budget.[60]

The Mike O'Callaghan–Pat Tillman Memorial Bridge did not open to traffic until October 20, 2010, some five years after construction began. Named in honor of former Nevada Governor Mike O'Callaghan and a soldier who died in Afghanistan after giving up a career in the NFL to join the fight against terrorism, the oft-delayed structure assumed its place as the world's longest and highest concrete arch bridge. At that point, through-traffic across Hoover Dam ended except for visitor travel to the Arizona-side parking lot.[61] The long tradition of driving across Hoover Dam—itself a form of tourist recreation—came to an end.

It is important to remember that many of the challenges LMNRA faced, in the 2000s and before, likely would not have occurred or have been as

FIGURE 5.7. The Mike O'Callaghan–Pat Tillman Memorial Bridge nearing completion in 2010. Courtesy of Marianne Molland.

severe on a natural lake in a wetter region. As they occurred relative to a reservoir of great strategic value in an arid region, the issues with mussels, cross-dam traffic, and drought attracted a stronger, much more rapid by the NPS than might have been the case elsewhere. Likewise, the area's proximity to large, urban areas in a desert climate virtually guaranteed overuse. NPS and LMNRA administrators adapted as best they could to these and other contextual stressors. In the end, however, there was no option other than increased regulation and limitation on recreational activity and access, which in turn ran counter to long-held public expectations regarding what the area should be. By the early twenty-first century, the days of free access, unlimited availability, and largely unregulated recreation on Lakes Mead and Mohave were over.

NOTES

1. "Are National Parks Becoming Crime Havens?" ABC News, 25 June 2003, http://abcnews.go.com/2020/story?id=123679 (accessed February 19, 2016).

2. Ralph Varagedian, "The Law Loses Out at U.S. National Parks," *Los Angeles Times*, 23 January 2003.

3. "Are National Parks Becoming Crime Havens?" ABC News, 25 June 2003.

4. Varagedian, "The Law Loses Out at U.S. National Parks."

5. Ibid.

6. Kurt Repanshek, "Violent Deaths in the National Parks," http://www.national parkstraveler.com/2008/03/violent-deaths-national-parks; Richard Simon and Judy Pasternak, "U.S. Considers Easing Ban on Guns in National Parks," *Los Angeles Times,* 23 February 2008.

7. "Las Vegas, Nevada: Crime Rates by Year," http://www.city-data.com/city/Las -Vegas-Nevada.html.

8. Richard West Sellars, *Preserving Nature in the National Parks: A History* (New Haven: Yale University Press, 1997), 22–23; David Louter, *Windshield Wilderness: Cars, Roads, and Nature in Washington's National Parks* (Seattle: University of Washington Press, 2006), 8–9.

9. Greg Lukianoff and Jonathan Haidt, "The Coddling of the American Mind," *Atlantic,* September 2015. http://www.theatlantic.com/magazine/archive/2015/09 /the-coddling-of-the-american-mind/399356/.

10. Henry Brean, "Anti-Graffiti Crew Cleans Up," *Las Vegas Review-Journal*, 3 October 2006; "Paintball Play Damages Petroglyphs, Rocks Near Laughlin," *Las Vegas Review-Journal*, 25 March 2010.

11. John Kimak, "2000 Statistics Reveal Lake Mead Rangers Kept Busy," *Las Vegas Review-Journal*, 17 June 2001.

12. Recreation visitation for 2001 was 8,465,547. National Park Service, "Lake Mead NRA," https://irma.nps.gov/Stats/SSRSReports/Park Specific Reports/Annual Park Recreation Visitation (1904 - Last Calendar Year)?Park=LAKE (accessed February 19, 2016).

13. Keith Rogers, "Lake Mead Fifth in Accidents, Report Says," *Las Vegas Review-Journal*, 6 September 2003; Lake Mead National Recreation Area, "Strategic Plan for Lake Mead National Recreation Area, 2001–2005" (Boulder City: Lake Mead National Recreation Area, 2000), 10, 29.

14. Mary Manning, "Better Cell Service Sought for Lake," *Las Vegas Sun*, 19 March 2004.

15. David McGrath Schwartz, "Authorities Putting Emphasis on Lake Safety," *Las Vegas Review-Journal*, 27 May 2006; Henry Brean, "Flying Rafts Out of Control," *Las Vegas Review-Journal*, 28 August 2006.

16. "American Watercraft Association to Protest Closure," Boats.com, http:// features.boats.com/boat-content/2002/08/american-watercraft-association-to -protest-closure/ (accessed January 5, 2015).

17. "Personal Watercraft Ban at Lake Mead Postponed," *Los Angeles Times,* 29 December 2002; "Effective Date on Personal Watercraft Closures Extended," Lake Mead National Recreation Area News Release, 6 September 2002; "Lake Mead to Ban Personal Watercraft," News Now, KLAS TV, 22 July 2002. http://search.8newsnow .com/default.aspx?ct=r&type=5,63;6,119;268,6843;361,75444;20599,91232845&pg=60 (accessed January 5, 2015).

18. Keith Rogers, "Plan Oks Personal Watercraft," *Las Vegas Review-Journal,* 9 January 2003; "Lake Mead National Recreation Area: Black Canyon Restrictions, Motorized Vessel Use-Willow Beach to Hoover Dam," http://nps.gov/lake/planyour visit/blackcanyonrestrictions.htm (accessed April 22, 2010); National Park Service,

"Personal Watercraft Use at Lake Mead National Recreation Area, Final Rule," 36 CFR Part 7, RIN 1024-AC91, Washington, D.C.: Department of the Interior, April 9, 2003, 4.

19. Keith Rogers, "Lake Mead Fee Collection Figures Show High Number of $5 Passes Sold," *Las Vegas Review-Journal*, 4 June 2001.

20. Keith Rogers, "Lake Mead User Fees Rising January 15," *Las Vegas Review-Journal*, 30 December 2010.

21. Keith Rogers, "Lake Mead Fees Could Rise," *Las Vegas Review-Journal*, 6 April 2010.

22. Don Martin, "Fee Increase Proposed for Lake Mead is Unfair," *Kingman Daily Miner*, 21 April 2010.

23. "Proposal Would Hike Fees for Lake Mead," *Boulder City Review*, 11 February 2015.

24. Wlfs4ever, Mojave Red, and iamthesmf, "National Recreation Area Proposes Fee Increases," Nevada General Fishing forum, http://www.bigfishtackle.com /forum/Nevada_Fishing_Forum_C39/Nevada_Fishing_General_F42/LAKE_MEAD _NATIONAL_RECREATION_AREA_PROPOSES_FEE_INCREASES_P919124/ (accessed February 17, 2015).

25. "Proposal Would Hike Fees for Lake Mead," *Boulder City Review*, 11 February 2015.

26. Kirk Johnson and Dean E. Murphy, "Drought Settles In, Lake Shrinks and West's Worries Grow," *New York Times*, 2 May 2004.

27. Felicity Barringer, "Lake Mead Hits Record Low Level," *New York Times*, 18 October 2010; National Park Service, "Storage Capacity of Lake Mead," http://www.nps .gov/lake/learn/nature/storage-capacity-of-lake-mead.htm (accessed February 22, 2016); "Lake Mead Water Levels Worry Observers," KLAS News, Las Vegas, Nevada, 9 April 2010, http://klas.dua1.worldnow.com/story/12286324/lake-mead-water-levels -worry-observers (accessed February 17, 2016).

28. Henry Brean, "Receding Water Strands Boaters at Lake's Northern Tip," *Las Vegas Review-Journal*, 24 April 2010.

29. National Park Service, "Overton Beach Impacted by Lowering Lake Levels," Press Release 65–06, Lake Mead National Recreation Area, 26 December 2006; Brean, "Receding Water Strands Boaters at Lake's Northern Tip."

30. "Park Officials Close Pearce Ferry Launch Ramp," *Las Vegas Review-Journal*, 26 August 2001; "Lake Vegas Bay Marina's Relocation to Horsepower Cove Begins," *Las Vegas Review-Journal*, 2 October 2002; Henry Brean, "Drought Keeps Marinas on the Move," *Las Vegas Review-Journal*, 7 February 2004.

31. Henry Brean, "Lake Mead is Ramping Up," *Las Vegas Review-Journal*, 8 August 2006; "Echo Bay Marina Move Set," *Las Vegas Review-Journal*, 28 February 2008.

32. Henry Brean, "Receding Lake Presents Challenges," *Las Vegas Review-Journal*, 21 March 2007.

33. Henry Brean, "Intake Work Stalls Again," *Las Vegas Review-Journal*, 1 December 2010; Henry Brean, "Focus on Lake Mead," *Las Vegas Review-Journal*, 20 April 2004.

34. Henry Brean, "Lake Sinking Near 1965 Level," *Las Vegas Review-Journal*, 14 April 2009.

35. "Third Drinking Water Intake at Lake Mead," Southern Nevada Water Authority, http://www.snwa.com/about/regional_intake3.html (accessed February 25, 2016); Henry Brean, "Historic Breakthrough at Lake Mead Comes During Water Board Meeting," *Las Vegas Review-Journal*, 10 December 2014.

36. Henry Brean, "Water on its way from new Lake Mead straw," *Las Vegas Review-Journal*, 23 September 2015; Ken Ritter, "Third Straw Uncapped to Provide Lake Mead Water to Vegas," AP, 23 September 2015, http://news.yahoo.com/third-straw-uncapped-lake-mead-water-vegas-033417377.html (accessed February 19, 2016).

37. Brean, "Receding Lake Presents Challenges."

38. Henry Brean, "Dam Relic emerges from Lake," *Las Vegas Review-Journal*, 7 June 2004.

39. Henry Brean, "Drought Uncovering Lake Artifacts," *Las Vegas Review-Journal*, 25 June 2004; "Editorial: Cultural Resources," *Las Vegas Review-Journal*, 28 June 2004.

40. Michael Wines, "States in Parched Southwest Take Steps to Bolster Lake Mead," *New York Times*, 17 December 2014.

41. "Water Worries: The Drying of the West," *Economist*, 27 January 2011.

42. William M. Welch, "West's Water Worries Rise as Lake Mead Falls," *USA Today*, 26 July 2014.

43. National Park Service, "Lake Mead NRA: Annual Park Recreation Visitation," https://irma.nps.gov/Stats/SSRSReports/Park%20Specific%20Reports/Annual%20Park%20Recreation%20Visitation%20%281904%20-%20Last%20Calendar%20Year%29?Park=LAKE (accessed February 12, 2015).

44. Stegeman, "Nevada Division of Environmental Protection Fact Sheet: Lake Mead Hatchery," 1; Eugene P. Moehring, *Resort City in the Sunbelt: Las Vegas, 1930–2000*, 2nd ed. (Reno: University of Nevada Press, 2000), 36.

45. Keith Rogers, "Lake's Invasive Mussel ID'd as Quagga," *Las Vegas Review-Journal*, 13 January 2007; "Live Zebra Mussels Found at Lake Mead," National Park Service News Release, January 10, 2007.

46. Keith Rogers, "Lake's Invasive Mussel ID'd as Quagga," *Las Vegas Review-Journal*, 13 January 2007; Keith Rogers, "Mussel Infestation Limited," *Las Vegas Review-Journal*, 17 January 2007.

47. "Live Zebra Mussels Found at Lake Mead," National Park Service News Release, January 10, 2007.

48. Stephanie Tavares, "Quagga Mussels a Toxic Threat to Lake Mead," *Las Vegas Sun*, 9 November 2009.

49. Keith Rogers, "Ranger Snares Invasive Mollusk," *Las Vegas Review-Journal*, 12 June 2004.

50. National Park Service, "Invasive Mussel Update from Lake Mead National Recreation Area," News Release No. 2–07, Lake Mead National Recreation Area, 16 January 2007; Keith Rogers, "Mussel Infestation Limited," *Las Vegas Review-Journal*, 17 January 2007; Henry Brean, "Invasive Mussel Found in Lake Mohave," *Las Vegas Review-Journal*, 23 January 2007.

51. Keith Rogers, "Multistate Quagga Containment Plan Considered," *Las Vegas Review-Journal*, 24 January 2007; Fred Love, "Official Urges Rapid-Response Tactics

to Curb Invasive Species," *Las Vegas Review-Journal,* 8 March 2007; Fred Love, "House OK's bill to Combat Invasive Species," *Las Vegas Review-Journal,* 20 March 2007.

52. "Invasive Mussels Threaten Lake Mead," MSNBC.com, 18 July 2009, http://www.msnbc.msn.com/id/31980811 (accessed April 23, 2010).

53. Ibid.

54. Keith Rogers, "Boaters Finding Mussels a Big Pain," *Las Vegas Review-Journal,* 3 March 2008.

55. Ibid.

56. "Plan to Kill Mountain Lions at Lake Mead Draws Protests," *Casper Star-Tribune,* 9 April 2006; Kurt Repanshek, "Lake Mead Mountain Lions," *National Park Traveler,* http://www.nationalparkstraveler.com/2006/04/lake-mead-mountain-lions (accessed Feb. 20, 2015); "Mountain Lions in Arizona's Line of Fire," *Las Vegas Sun,* 7 April 2006.

57. Keith Rogers, "Threats to Hoover Dam Assessed," *Las Vegas Review Journal,* 16 September 2001; Michael Squires, "Hoover Dam Bypass: Officials See Need for Speed," *Las Vegas Review-Journal,* 2 October 2001; Christine Dorsey, "Hoover Dam Bypass: State Leaders Reiterate Need to Build Quickly," *Las Vegas Review-Journal,* 28 February 2002.

58. Michael Squires, "Hoover Dam Bypass: Work on Project Begins," *Las Vegas Review-Journal,* 22 October 2002.

59. Henry Brean, "Hoover Bypass About to Get Off the Ground," *Las Vegas Review-Journal,* 17 December 2005; "Contract for Bypass Awarded," *Las Vegas Review-Journal,* 2 November 2004.

60. Omar Sofradzija, "Dam Bypass Looking Up," *Las Vegas Review-Journal,* 19 August 2006; Omar Sofradzija, "Two-Year Delay at Dam," *Las Vegas Review-Journal,* 25 January 2007.

61. Tony Illia, "Bridge to Tomorrow," *Las Vegas Review-Journal,* 19 April 2009; Adrienne Packer, "Bridge to Open to Traffic Sans Fanfare," *Las Vegas Review-Journal,* 20 October 2010; Adrienne Packer, "Hoover Dam Bypass Bridge Opens," *Las Vegas Review-Journal,* 21 October 2010.

Conclusion
Maintaining the Pace?

Walking along the top of Hoover Dam, I am struck by the immensity of both the natural and the man-made surroundings. It is an overwhelming experience of extreme contrasts made possible by monumental undertakings. There is the stark yet sublime power of concrete and steel holding back unimaginable forces of water. And the water itself, against desert mountains and burning sun, almost defies human comprehension. The view always leaves me feeling conflicted. I feel at once powerful by virtue of belonging to such a capable and innovative people, and yet embarrassed by our hubris in thinking that such domination of nature can solve our problems and stand permanently.

The view from Hoover Dam also speaks of a history that is no less conflicted and overwhelming. It is a story filled with significance, progress, victory, and tragedy. That history is the real backdrop for the boaters who skim across the lake today. They do so because of the reclamation-era determination—be it right or wrong—to transform nature and propel a region. Because of such determination and the beliefs that supported it, this first national recreation area came into existence as Uncle Sam gained his first playground. In accepting management over this altered waterscape, the NPS assumed a role as mediator of reservoir-based recreation in the arid West's modern hydraulic society.

Yet the activities on display also present much more than the end result of a new administrative designation created within the NPS so many decades ago. They are, instead, the most recent product of a complex and lengthy interaction of people with the natural and the built landscape, with each other, and with their government. From its wild and muddy river origins to its deep and clear present, water has shaped that story. As a result, the Lake Mead National Recreation Area is an extraordinarily significant historical place. It is the epicenter where water's transformation has spurred mass recreation, regional growth, environmental transformation, and raw power.

It is also the area where such forces have been compelled to coexist and this has inspired reactions.

It is important to remember that the water's transformation did not occur in an empty landscape, and the process was both physical and intellectual. For where the recreationists now seek pleasure, others once sought livelihoods, raised families, conquered, and were conquered. Through successive generations, they lived, died, and experienced all the joys and tribulations that define life. An important and undeniable part of that life today and in this area is outdoor recreation. That the federal government has shaped our interactions and expectations concerning outdoor recreation is one lesson of Lake Mead. Those expectations and interactions remain controversial, contested, and deeply cherished. They are a product of the transformation of water that has happened here.

Lake Mead's influence on water-based outdoor recreation is strikingly apparent. For over one hundred years, Americans have been utilizing government reclamation projects for water-based recreational activities. And for most of that time Americans have been doing so at sprawling, government-managed NRAs. The power of the state was seemingly invisible as limitations on access and regulations on behavior were few. Prior to the 2000s, many people had only experienced the Colorado River in this manner. To them, the reservoir *was* nature, and their use of it was convenient and largely without cost or limit. The recreation area and its reservoirs subsequently assumed a central place in their concept of outdoor recreational activity. Over time, generations came to view such interaction as a right, with the government's role merely that of ensuring convenience of use. They have, in the process, taken for granted the government's ability to provide easily accessible, safe, and largely free water-based outdoor recreation. Here, we should not be surprised that recreationists will seek to protect their endeavors when challenges to accessibility reveal those endeavors' tenuous reality. We also should not be surprised at the NPS's difficulties in managing reservoir-based recreation.

In this way too, the area has been a pacesetter. Today, for better and for worse, the experiences and expectations of the 44,679,478 annual visitors to the various NRAs are shaped by what has occurred here.[1] As the national recreation area system and the ideas associated with it emerged during the reclamation era, LMNRA's story is, at base, one in which an area's perceived usefulness increased through environmental transformation. Early on, NPS management of a transformed, resource-oriented landscape as a large playground seemed to work. To hundreds of thousands and then millions of urban and suburban recreationists, LMNRA provided the outdoor recreational needs they sought and increasingly believed they deserved. Yet as urban populations grew, usage increased, technology advanced, recreation diversified, and attitudes toward nature and its enjoyment shifted. With these shifts, reservoir-based recreational experience became more controversial, contested, and, for the government, expensive. Cracks in the future of the hydraulic society subsequently became more apparent.

In creating LMNRA and the NRAs that followed in its image, lawmakers set up a worthwhile but challenging and labor-intensive system. By agreeing to manage this system, the NPS took on the nearly impossible task of providing safe, accessible recreational experiences for the people in inherently dangerous, large, increasingly crowded, and environmentally marginal areas. At Lake Mead, this has meant dealing with incredibly high visitation rates, an increasingly risk-averse public's perception of danger and crime in the area, plus a host of environmental issues that require reduced recreational accessibility and ever-more-regulated behavior.

Balancing it all became exceedingly difficult in a time when budget cuts, government gridlock, and safety consciousness defined the American political norm. Former LMNRA Supervisor Alan O'Neill recently pointed out that the entire NPS received approximately one-fourteenth of 1 percent of the annual federal budget. Although largely inconsequential in terms of overall government expenditures or deficit reduction, the NPS budgetary allotment is one of the first on the chopping block when calls for fiscal responsibility echo through the halls of Congress. O'Neill likened the budget of the NPS and other Department of the Interior agencies as "low-hanging fruit" when budget cutters come calling.[2]

This is particularly mind-boggling when one considers the return on investment at NPS units such as LMNRA. According to the NPS, every dollar invested in park operations generates approximately ten dollars, while every two park-service jobs tend to yield at least one additional job outside of the service. It was estimated that in 2012 alone, LMNRA generated more than $406 million in sales for the surrounding area and almost 4,000 jobs. At the same time, the NPS suffered from an annual operations shortfall of approximately $500 to $600 million. Much of this shortfall was the result of increased expenditures and budget cuts of some 15 percent over the preceding decade. Such reductions and shortfalls were definitely felt at LMNRA, where the preceding five years witnessed the loss of a dozen staff positions.[3] Considering such numbers, O'Neill questioned where LMNRA and, by association, other NPS units were headed. Such cuts, he posited, would inevitably result in less protection and fewer amenities for visitors. Eventually, he suggested, "There will be no one there" in the areas that "define what's special about America."[4]

But beyond the dollars and cents of it all, recreating at LMNRA and other NRAs remains a very important aspect of many people's lives. For example, in 2013, when the government shut down temporarily due to political squabbling and inability to compromise, visitors to LMNRA found its gates locked. In response, Stuart Litjens, owner of the Boulder Boats dealership, organized a protest. In an effort to draw attention to the closure and loss of recreational accessibility, he urged LMNRA recreationists to hook up their trailered boats for a protest convoy down the Las Vegas Strip. People obliged, slowly driving down the strip with boats in tow, honking their horns, and displaying colorful signs protesting the closure. Speaking for the protestors, Litjens said, "We're upset with the [government] shutdown" and just "want to be on [Lake Mead] with our families."[5]

The NPS has done a remarkable job in recent decades of allowing Americans to continue to be on the lake with their families, despite the increasingly challenging context surrounding reservoir-based recreation. So far, it has lived up to the expectations created and fostered during the first decades of LMNRA's existence. However, those expectations are largely unrealistic and quite possibly untenable in a future that promises exponential increase in popular demand crashing against an ever more limited resource. Early on, mistakes were made in setting public expectation regarding reservoir-based recreation in arid lands. Such ideas are now, however, deeply embedded and are what the NPS and nation must live with heading into the future. In that future, recreationists' entrenched ideas about reservoir-based recreation will continue to run up against a changing climate, increased concern with safety and preservation, and the conflicting interests of a more varied constituency. As this occurs, the NPS's ability to meet recreationists' demands can only become even more difficult, as more stringent regulation of activities and accessibility becomes necessary. In turn, the future of an extravagant oasis lifestyle upon which the modern hydraulic society rests becomes all the more precarious.

NOTES

1. National Park Service, "Annual Park Recreation Visitation," https://irma.nps .gov/Stats/SSRSReports/Park%20Specific%20Reports/Annual%20Park%20Rec reation%20Visitation%20%281904%20-%20Last%20Calendar%20Year%29?Park =LAKE (accessed February 10, 2015).

2. Henry Brean, "National Parks Bracing for Cuts," *Las Vegas Review-Journal,* 10 December 2012.

3. Ibid.; Alan O'Neill, "Protect Lake Mead and the Legacy of the National Parks," *Las Vegas Sun,* 29 December 2012.

4. O'Neill, "Protect Lake Mead and the Legacy of the National Parks," *Las Vegas Sun.*

5. Rochel Leah Goldblatt, "Boats Roll on Strip to Protest Lake Mead Closure," *Las Vegas Review-Journal,* 6 October 2013.

Bibliography

BOOKS AND ARTICLES

Alley, John R. Jr. "Prelude to Dispossession: The Fur Trade's Significance for the Northern Utes and Southern Paiutes." *Utah Historical Quarterly* 50 (spring 1982): 104–23.

Arrington, Leonard J. "Inland to Zion: Mormon Trade on the Colorado River, 1864–1867." *Arizona and the West* 8 (autumn 1966):239–50.

Bancroft, Hubert. *History of Arizona and New Mexico: 1530–1888.* Albuquerque: Horn & Wallace, 1962.

Barlowe, Raleigh. "Past, Present, and Future Demand for Land for Recreation." *Agricultural History* 36 (October 1962):230–31.

Belshaw, Mike and Ed Peplow Jr. *Historic Resources Study: Lake Mead National Recreation Area, Nevada.* Denver: National Park Service, 1980.

Billingsley, George. "Prospector's Proving Ground: Mining and the Grand Canyon." *Journal of Arizona History* 17 (winter 1976):69–88.

Bishop, M. Guy. "Mission 66 in the National Parks of Southern California and the Southwest." *Southern California Quarterly* 80 (fall 1998):293–314.

Brennan, Irene J., ed. *Fort Mojave, 1859–1890: Letters of the Commanding Officers.* Manhattan, KS: Military Affairs/Aerospace History Publishing, 1980.

Briggs, Carl and Clyde Francis Trudell. *Quarterdeck & Saddlehorn: The Story of Edward F. Beale, 1822–1893.* Glendale, CA: Arthur H. Clark Company, 1983.

Carr, Ethan. *Mission 66: Modernism and the National Parks Dilemma.* Amherst: University of Massachusetts Press, 2007.

Casebier, Dennis G. *Camp El Dorado, Arizona Territory: Soldiers, Steamboats, and Miners on the Upper Colorado River.* Tempe: Arizona Historical Foundation, 1970.

Cline, Gloria Griffen. *Exploring the Great Basin.* Reno: University of Nevada Press, 1988.

Cordell, H. Ken and Gegory R. Super, "Trends in Americans' Outdoor Recreation." In *Trends in Outdoor Recreation, Leisure, and Tourism,* edited by William C. Gartner and David W. Lime, 133–44. Wallingford, UK: CABI Publishing, 2000.

D'Antuono, Karen. "The National Park Service's Proposed Ban: A New Approach to Personal Watercraft Use in the National Parks." *Boston College Environmental Affairs Law Review* 27 (2000):243–78.

Dodd, Douglas W. "Boulder Dam Recreation Area: The Bureau of Reclamation, the National Park Service, and the Origins of the National Recreation Area Concept at Lake Mead, 1929–1936." In *The Bureau of Reclamation: History Essays from the Centennial Symposium*, edited by Brit Allan Storey. Denver: U.S. Bureau of Reclamation, 2008.

———. "Boulder Dam Recreation Area: The Bureau of Reclamation, The National Park Service, and the Origins of the National Recreation Area Concept at Lake Mead, 1929–1936." *Southern California Quarterly* 88 (winter 2006–2007):431–73.

Dulles, Foster Rhea. *A History of Recreation: America Learns to Play.* New York: Appleton-Century Crofts, 1965.

Dunbar, Andrew J., and Dennis McBride. *Building Hoover Dam: An Oral History of the Great Depression.* New York: Twayne Publishers, 1993.

Euler, Robert C. "Southern Paiute Ethnohistory." *University of Utah Anthropological Papers* 78 (April 1966).

Ezzo, Joseph A. *A Class I Cultural Resources Survey of the Moapa and Virgin Valley, Clark County Nevada.* Statistical Research Technical Series 58. Report submitted to USDI Bureau of Reclamation Lower Colorado Region, 1996.

Farmer, Jared. *Glen Canyon Dammed: Inventing Lake Powell and the Canyon Country.* Tucson: University of Arizona Press, 1999.

Flink, James J. "Three Stages of Automobile Consciousness." *American Quarterly* 24 (October 1972):451–73.

———. *The Automobile Age.* Cambridge: MIT Press, 1990.

Foreman, Grant. *A Pathfinder in the Southwest: The Itinerary of Lieutenant A. W. Whipple During His Explorations for a Railway Route from Fort Smith to Los Angeles in the Years 1853 and 1854.* Norman: University of Oklahoma Press, 1941.

Glennon, Robert. *Unquenchable: America's Water Crisis and What To Do About It.* Washington, D.C.: Island Press, 2009.

———. *Water Follies: Groundwater Pumping and the Fate of America's Fresh Waters.* Washington, D.C.: Island Press, 2002.

Glennon, Robert, Gabriel Eckstein, Hussein A. Amery, Dan Keppen, and Steve Werner. "Turning on the Tap: The World's Water Problems." *Frontiers in Ecology and the Environment* 9 (November 2005):503–09.

Greenfield, Steven. "A Lake by Mistake." *American Heritage of Invention and Technology* 21 (winter 2006):38–49.

Hafen, LeRoy and Ann W. Hafen. *Old Spanish Trail: Santa Fe to Los Angeles.* Glendale: Arthur H. Clark Company, 1954.

Hine, Robert V., and John Mack Faragher. *The American West: An Interpretive History.* New Haven: Yale University Press, 2000.

Hoffman, Alice Margaret. "The Evolution of the Highway from Salt Lake City to Los Angeles." MA thesis, University of Southern California, 1936.

Hosmer, Helen. "Imperial Valley: Triumph and Failure in the Colorado Desert." *The American West* 3 (winter 1966):34–49.

Huber, Edgar K. "Hualapai Bay Archaeology: Class II Noncollection Cultural Resource Survey along the Eastern Arm of Lake Mead, Mohave County, Arizona." Tucson: Statistical Research.

Hundley, Norris Jr. *Water and the West: The Colorado River Compact and the Politics of Water in the American West.* Berkeley: University of California Press, 1975.

Hunter, Milton R. "The Mormons and the Colorado River." *American Historical Review* 44 (April 1939):549–55.

Jaeger, Edmund C. *The North American Deserts.* Stanford: Stanford University Press, 1957.

Kelly, Isabel T., and Catherine S. Fowler. "Southern Paiute." In *Handbook of North American Indians, Vol. 11: Great Basin,* edited by Warren L. D'Azevedo. Washington, D.C.: Smithsonian Institution, 1983.

Knack, Martha C. *Boundaries Between: The Southern Paiutes, 1775–1995.* Lincoln: University of Nebraska Press, 2001.

Larson, Peggy and Lane Larson. *The Deserts of the Southwest: A Sierra Club Naturalist's Guide.* 2nd ed. San Francisco: Sierra Club Books, 1997.

Lear, Linda J. "Boulder Dam: A Crossroads in Natural Resource Policy." *Journal of the West* 24 (October 1985):82–94.

Leavitt, Francis H. "Steam Navigation on the Colorado River." *California Historical Society Quarterly* 22 (March 1943):1–25.

Louter, David. *Windshield Wilderness: Cars, Roads, and Nature in Washington's National Parks.* Seattle: University of Washington Press, 2006.

McBride, Dennis. "Grand Canyon-Boulder Dam Tours, Inc.: Southern Nevada's First Venture into Commercial Tourism." *Nevada Historical Society Quarterly* 27 (summer 1984):92–108.

McClintock, James H. *Mormon Settlement in Arizona: A Record of Peaceful Conquest of the Desert.* Phoenix, 1921.

McMillen, Christian W. *Making Indian Law: The Hualapai Land Case and the Birth of Ethnohistory.* New Haven: Yale University Press, 2007.

Miller, David H. "The Ives Expedition Revisited: A Prussian's Impressions." *Journal of Arizona History* 13 (spring 1972):1–25.

Moehring, Eugene. "Las Vegas and the Second World War." *Nevada Historical Society Quarterly* 29 (spring 1986):1–30.

Officer, James E. *Hispanic Arizona, 1536–1856.* Tucson: University of Arizona Press, 1987.

Paher, Stanley W. *Callville: Head of Navigation.* Las Vegas: Nevada Publications, undated. UNLV Special Collections. Call# F 811 C34.

———. *Nevada Ghost Towns and Mining Camps.* Berkeley: Howell-North Books, 1970.

Pisani, Donald J. "Federal Reclamation and the American West." *Agricultural History* 77 (summer 2003):291–320.

———. *To Reclaim a Divided West: Water, Law, and Public Policy, 1848–1902.* Albuquerque: University of New Mexico Press, 1992.

Price, Virginia and John T. Darby. "Preston Nutter: Utah Cattleman, 1886–1936." *Utah Historical Quarterly* 32 (summer 1964):232–51.

Rae, John B. *The Road and the Car in American Life.* Cambridge: MIT Press, 1971.

Reisner, Marc. *Cadillac Desert: The American West and Its Disappearing Water.* Revised and updated edition. New York: Penguin, 1993.

Reisner, Marc and Sarah Bates. *Overtapped Oasis: Reform or Revolution for Western Water.* Washington, D.C.: Island Press, 1990.

Riggs, John L. "The Reign of Violence in El Dorado Canyon." *Third Biennial Report of the Nevada State Historical Society* (1913):95–107.

Ronda, James. "Passion and Imagination in the Exploration of the American West." In *A Companion to the American West,* edited by William Deverell, 53–76. Malden, MA: Blackwell, 2004.

Rothman, Hal. "Administrative History of the Lake Mead National Recreation Area." Unpublished manuscript in author's possession.

———. *The New Urban Park: Golden Gate National Recreation Area and Civic Environmentalism.* Lawrence: University Press of Kansas, 2004.

Sellars, Richard West. *Preserving Nature in the National Parks: A History.* New Haven: Yale University Press, 1997.

Smith, Melvin T. "Colorado River Exploration and the Mormon War." *Utah Historical Quarterly* 38 (summer 1970):207–23.

Smith, Thomas G. "John Kennedy, Stewart Udall, and New Frontier Conservation." *Pacific Historical Review* 64 (August 1995):329–62.

Spicer, Edward H. *Cycles of Conquest: The Impact of Spain, Mexico, and the United States on the Indians of the Southwest, 1533–1960.* Tucson: University of Arizona Press, 1962.

Splett, James. "Personal Watercraft Use: A Nationwide Problem Requiring Local Regulation." *Journal of Environmental Law and Regulation* 14 (1999):185–224.

Stevens, Joseph E. *Hoover Dam: An American Adventure.* Norman: University of Oklahoma Press, 1988.

Stewart, Kenneth M. "The Mohave Indians of Hispanic Times." *Kiva* 22 (October 1966):25–38.

Townley, J. M. "Early Development of Eldorado Canyon and Searchlight Mining Districts." *Nevada Historical Society Quarterly* 11, no. 1 (spring 1968):1–25.

Wagoner, Jay J. *Early Arizona: Prehistory to Civil War.* Tucson: University of Arizona Press, 1975.

Wallace, Andrew. "Across Arizona to the Big Colorado: The Sitgreaves Expedition of 1851." *Arizona and the West* 26 (winter 1984):325–64.

Ward, Diane Raines. *Water Wars: Drought, Flood, Folly, and the Politics of Thirst.* New York: Penguin, 2002.

Weber, David J. *The Mexican Frontier, 1821–1846: The American Southwest Under Mexico.* Albuquerque: University of New Mexico Press, 1982.

Wittfogel, Karl A. *Oriental Despotism: A Comparative Study of Total Power.* New Haven: Yale University Press.

Woerner, Lloyd. "The Creation of the Salton Sea: An Engineering Folly." *Journal of the West* 28 (January 1989):109–12.

Worster, Donald. "Hoover Dam: A Study in Domination." In *Under Western Skies: Nature and History in the American West*, 64–78. New York: Oxford University Press, 1992.

———. "Hydraulic Society in California." In *Under Western Skies: Nature and History in the American West*, 53–63. New York: Oxford University Press, 1992.

———. *Rivers of Empire: Water, Aridity, and the Growth of the American West*. New York: Oxford University Press, 1992.

THESES AND DISSERTATIONS

Braithwaite, Douglas Charles. "The Mastery of Cultural Contradictions: Developing Paiute Indian Leadership." PhD diss., Massachusetts Institute of Technology, 1971.

Leavitt, Francis H. "Influence of the Mormon People in the Settlement of Clark County." MA thesis, University of Nevada, Reno, 1934.

Smith, Melvin T. "The Colorado River: Its History in the Lower Canyons Area." PhD diss., Brigham Young University, Provo, UT, 1972.

DIARIES, JOURNALS, EXCERPTS

Garcés, Francisco. *A Record of Travels in Arizona and California, 1775–1776*. Translated and edited by John Galvin. San Francisco: John Howell Books, 1965.

———. *On the Trail of a Spanish Pioneer: Diary and Itinerary of Francisco Garcés in His Travels Through Sonora, Arizona, and California, 1775–1776*. Translated by Elliot Coues. New York: Francis P. Harper, 1900.

Möllhausen, Balduin. *Diary of a Journal from the Mississippi to the Coasts of the Pacific With a United States Government Expedition*. Translated by Mrs. Percy Sinnett. London: Longman, Brown, Green, Longmans, & Roberts, 1858.

GOVERNMENT DOCUMENTS AND REPORTS

Banister, Earl W. "Active Work Projects: Camp NP–6, Boulder City, Nevada," 28 September 1938. Box Civilian Conservation Corps (CCC) Nevada: Camp Inspection Reports, Folder Civilian Conservation Corps (CCC)—Nevada: Boulder City, Nevada, 1935–1941, Camp No. NP–6. UNLV Special Collections.

Beale, Edward F. *The Report of the Superintendent of the Wagon Road from Fort Defiance to the Colorado River*. H.R. Doc. No. 35-124 (May 12, 1858).

Committee Appointed by the Associated General Contractors of America and the American Engineering Council. "Report on Hoover Dam Project and Present Status." December 1931.

"Grand Canyon-Parashant National Monument: Records of Decision and Resource Management Plan/General Management Plan." Bureau of Land Management/National Park Service. February 2008

Ingalls, G. W. "Pai-Ute Agency, Nevada, October 1, 1874." In Commissioner of Indian Affairs Edward P. Smith, "Annual Report of the Commissioner of Indian Affairs to the Secretary of Interior for the Year 1874." Washington: Government Printing Office, 1874.

Ives, Joseph C. *Report Upon the Colorado River of the West in 1857 and 1858.* S. Doc., 36th Cong., 1st Sess. Washington D.C., 1861.

Jackson-Retondo, Elaine. "National Register of Historic Places Multiple Property Documentation Form, Lake Mead National Recreation Area Mission 66 Resources." Oakland: National Park Service, Pacific West Region, 2007.

Lake Mead National Recreation Area. "Strategic Plan for Lake Mead National Recreation Area, 2001–2005." Boulder City: Lake Mead National Recreation Area, 2000.

"Letter From the Acting Secretary of the Interior Transmitting the Reclamation Report on the Bulls Head Dam Project on the Colorado River Where that Stream Forms the Boundary Between Arizona and Nevada." H.R. Doc. 77-186 (April 28, 1941).

Mackun, Paul and Steven Wilson. "Population Distribution and Change, 2000–2010." Washington, D.C.: Department of Commerce, 2011.

McArthur, Aaron J. "Centrally Isolated: St. Thomas, Nevada." Historic Resource Study. Washington, D.C.: National Park Service, 2009.

National Park Service. "Personal Watercraft Use at Lake Mead National Recreation Area, Final Rule." 36 CFR Part 7, RIN 1024-AC91, Washington, D.C.: Department of the Interior (April 9, 2003).

Reddoch, J. C. "Supplementary Report: Camp SP–6, Company 2536, Boulder City, Nevada," 5 February 1937. Box Civilian Conservation Corps (CCC) Nevada: Camp Inspection Reports, Folder Civilian Conservation Corps (CCC)—Nevada: Boulder City, Nevada, 1935–1941, Camp No. NP–6. UNLV Special Collections.

Sitgreaves, Lorenzo. *Report of an Expedition down the Zuni and Colorado Rivers.* S. Doc. No. 32-59. Washington D.C. (1853).

Stegeman, E. Samuel. "Nevada Division of Environmental Protection Fact Sheet: Lake Mead Hatchery." Reno: Nevada Department of Wildlife, 2009.

United States Bureau of the Census. "Historical Statistics of the United States, Colonial Times to 1970: Part 1." Washington, D.C.: Department of Commerce, 1975.

United States Bureau of the Census. "Profile of General Demographic Characteristics: 2000." Washington, D.C.: United States Bureau of the Census, 2000.

———. "Nevada: Population of Counties by Decennial Census, 1900 to 1990." Compiled and edited by Richard L. Forstall. Washington, D.C., 1990.

United States Senate. "Problems of Imperial Valley and Vicinity." S. Doc. No. 67-142 (February 23, 1922).

Whipple, Amiel W. *Explorations and Surveys to Ascertain the Most Practical and Economical Route for a Railway from the Mississippi.* S. Doc. No. 33-78. Washington, D.C. (1856).

Whipple, Amiel W. *Report of Explorations for a Railway Route, near the Thirty-Fifth Parallel of Latitude from the Mississippi River to the Pacific Ocean.* H.R. Doc. No. 33-129. Washington, D.C. (1855).

LAWS, ACTS, AND PROCLAMATIONS

Boulder Canyon Project Act. Pub. L. No. 70–642, 45 Stat. 1057 (1928).

Grant, President Ulysses S. Executive Order. 12 February 1874. Sandovich Collection, Folder 2, UNLV Special Collections.

Hoover, Herbert. Proclamation No. 1882 (June 25, 1929), Colorado River Compact and the Boulder Canyon Project.

Lands in Severalty to Indians. Pub. L. No. 49-119, 24 Stat. 388 (Feb. 8, 1887).

Memorandum of Agreement Between the National Park Service and the Bureau of Reclamation. Relating to the Development and Administration of the Boulder Canyon Project Area, 29 August 1936. 1. Lake Mead National Recreation Area Folder, Boulder City/Hoover Dam Museum, Boulder City, Nevada.

National Park Service Organic Act of 1916 (16 U.S.C. l 2 3, and 4) August 25, 1916 (39 Stat. 535).

Reclamation Act of 1902 (U.S. Pub. L. No. 161).

Recreation Advisory Council. "Federal Executive Branch Policy Governing the Selection, Establishment, and Administration of National Recreational Areas," March 26, 1963. In *America's National Parks: The Critical Documents*, edited by Lary M. Dilsaver. New York: Rowman & Littlefield, 1994.

Yellowstone Park Act. 17 Stat. 32 (March 1, 1872).

ORAL HISTORIES

Ferguson, Edna Jackson. Interview in Andrew J. Dunbar and Dennis McBride, *Building Hoover Dam: An Oral History of the Great Depression.* New York: Twayne, 1993.

Young, Walker. Interview in Andrew J. Dunbar and Dennis McBride, *Building Hoover Dam: An Oral History of the Great Depression.* New York: Twayne, 1993.

PAMPHLETS, NEWSLETTERS, AND MISCELLANEOUS PRINTED MEDIA

Boulder Dam Postcard Booklet. Chicago: Curt Teich & Co., 1935.

Erikson, C. E. *Sunset Sportsman's Atlas: Colorado River and Lake Mead: Boating, Fishing, Exploring.* Menlo Park, CA: Lane Publishing, 1952.

TWA Advertisement. "The Joy's in the Journey," 1946.

United States Bureau of Reclamation. "Boulder Dam," pamphlet, Washington, D.C.: Department of the Interior, 1940s.

———. "Construction of Boulder Dam," Washington, D.C.: Department of the Interior, n.d. (1930s).

United States Department of the Interior, National Park Service.

"A Study of the Park and Recreation Problem of the United States," supplemental foreword. Washington, D.C.: U.S. Government Printing Office, 1941.

———. "Boulder Dam National Recreation Area: Arizona and Nevada." 1940.

———. "Boulder Dam National Recreation Area: Arizona and Nevada." Denver: W. H. Kistler Stationery Company, 1941.

———. "Lake Mead National Recreation Area: Arizona and Nevada: Lake Mead and Lake Mohave." Washington, D.C.: U.S. Government Printing Office, 1956.

———. "Lake Mead National Recreation Area: Arizona and Nevada: Lake Mead and Lake Mohave." Washington, D.C.: U.S. Government Printing Office, 1961.

———. "Lake Mead National Recreation Area: Mohave-Arizona-Nevada, Lake Mead-Arizona-Nevada." Washington, D.C.: U.S. Government Printing Office, 1964.

United States Department of the Interior. "The Sculptures at Boulder Dam," May 1942. UNLV Special Collections, Call# NB237 H25 A49 1942.

United States Postal Service. Three-Cent Stamp, 1935.

PERSONAL CORRESPONDENCE

Clum, H. R. Commissioner of Indian Affairs to Secretary of the Interior C. Delano. 7 March 1873. Sandovich Collection, Folder 2, UNLV Special Collections.

Cowen, B. R. Acting Secretary of the Interior to Commissioner of Indian Affairs E. P. Smith, 14 February 1874. Sandovich Collection, Folder 2, UNLV Special Collections.

POPULAR MAGAZINE AND NEWSPAPER ARTICLES

(Unsigned articles are alphabetical by title.)

"All Tourist Records Fall On Week End." *Las Vegas Evening Review-Journal,* 12 February 1934.

"Bad Wash-Out Caused by Cloudburst." *Boulder City Reminder,* 13 September 1939.

Baldwin, Gordon C. "The Lake Becomes a Playground." *Arizona Highways,* July 1946, 25.

Barringer, Felicity. "Lake Mead Hits Record Low Level." *New York Times,* 18 October 2010.

Bassett, James E. Jr. "Davis Dam, Fourth in Colorado Chain, Promises Rich Development." *Los Angeles Times,* 23 April 1946.

"Bathing Beach at Dam Lake is Being Built." *Las Vegas Evening Review-Journal,* 8 April 1936.

Benton, Liz. "Park Service Studying Hacienda Casino Purchase." *Las Vegas Review-Journal,* 28 October 2003.

Blair, William M. "Saving the Parks." *New York Times,* 12 February 1956.

Bloemhof, Alexander. "Company Lobbies for Chance to Build Lake Mead Plant." *Las Vegas Review-Journal,* 2 May 1993.

"Boulder CCC Camp Now Numbers 500." *Las Vegas Evening Review-Journal,* 16 January 1936.

"Boulder Dam Bill Sent to Coolidge." *New York Times,* 19 December 1928.

"Boulder Dam Bill Passes the Senate." *New York Times,* 15 December 1928.

"Boulder Dam Job Completed 2 Years Ahead of Schedule." *Las Vegas Evening Review-Journal,* 20 September 1935.

"Boulder Lake 84 Miles Long." *Las Vegas Evening Review-Journal,* 29 July 1935.

"Boulder Lake Holding Its Own." *Las Vegas Evening Review-Journal,* 31 July 1935.

Brean, Henry. "Anti-Graffiti Crew Cleans Up." *Las Vegas Review-Journal,* 3 October 2006.

———."BLM Wants Casino to Cash Out." *Las Vegas Review-Journal,* 16 February 2004.

———. "Dam Relic Emerges from Lake." *Las Vegas Review-Journal,* 7 June 2004.

———. "Drought Keeps Marinas on the Move." *Las Vegas Review-Journal,* 7 February 2004.

———. "Drought Uncovering Lake Artifacts." *Las Vegas Review-Journal,* 25 June 2004.

———. "Flying Rafts Out of Control." *Las Vegas Review-Journal,* 28 August 2006.

———. "Focus on Lake Mead." *Las Vegas Review-Journal,* 20 April 2004.

———. Historic Breakthrough at Lake Mead Comes During Water Board Meeting." *Las Vegas Review-Journal,* 10 December 2014.

———. "Hoover Bypass About to Get off the Ground." *Las Vegas Review-Journal,* 17 December 2005.

———. "Intake Work Stalls Again." *Las Vegas Review-Journal,* 1 December 2010.

———. "Invasive Mussel Found in Lake Mohave." *Las Vegas Review-Journal,* 23 January 2007.

———. "Lake Mead Is Ramping Up." *Las Vegas Review-Journal,* 8 August 2006.

———. "Lake Sinking Near 1965 Level." *Las Vegas Review-Journal,* 14 April 2009.

———. "National Parks Bracing for Cuts." *Las Vegas Review-Journal,* 10 December 2012.

———. "Receding Lake Presents Challenges." *Las Vegas Review-Journal,* 21 March 2007.

———. "Receding Water Strands Boaters at Lake's Northern Tip." *Las Vegas Review-Journal,* 24 April 2010.

———. "Water On Its Way From New Lake Mead Straw." *Las Vegas Review-Journal,* 23 September 2015.

"California: El Dorado Canyon." *Arizona Miner,* 18 July 1868.

Carlson, Raymond. "The Blue Waters of Lake Mead and Mohave." *Arizona Highways,* May 1964.

"CCC To Cease in Boulder City Next Tuesday." *Boulder City News,* 23 July 1942.

"Chief Says Parks Get Best of Care." *New York Times,* 30 August 1930.

"Closing Out of CCC Program Complete Work Revisited." *Boulder City News,* 28 August 1942.

"Colorado Desert Blooms." *New York Times,* 28 December 1902.

"Colorado River Diverted for Construction of Davis Dam." *Los Angeles Times,* 28 June 1948.

"Colorado River Tamed Today." *Las Vegas Evening Review-Journal,* 1 February 1935.

"Contract for Bypass Awarded." *Las Vegas Review-Journal,* 2 November 2004.

"Dam Destined to Grow as Tourist Hub." *Las Vegas Evening Review-Journal,* 10 January 1934.

"Davis Dam Almost Ready." *Los Angeles Times,* 19 December 1950.

"Davis Dam Open Friday." *New York Times,* 2 January 1951.

"Davis Dam Power Use Starts Friday." *Los Angeles Times,* 2 January 1951.

"Davis Dam Ready on Colorado River." *New York Times,* 4 December 1949.

"Davis Dam to Impound Water Late this Week." *Los Angeles Times,* 29 November 1949.

"Death of Dr. Wozencraft." *Daily Evening Bulletin,* 24 November 1887.

"Dedication Set for Davis Dam." *Los Angeles Times,* 28 November 1952.

"Demand on Harriman Made By President." *New York Times,* 21 December 1906.

Ditzel, Paul. "A Dam Site: Better Than an Unleashed River." *Westways* 68 (November 1976).

Dorsey, Christine. "Hoover Dam Bypass: State Leaders Reiterate Need to Build Quickly." *Las Vegas Review-Journal,* 28 February 2002.

"Dr. O. M. Wozencraft; Cortes." *Daily Democratic State Journal,* 28 June 1855.

"Echo Bay Marina Move Set." *Las Vegas Review-Journal,* 28 February 2008.

"Editorial: Cultural Resources." *Las Vegas Review-Journal,* 28 June 2004.

Edwards, Guy D. "Lake Recreational Development Carried on by CCC." *Las Vegas Evening Review-Journal,* 22 April 1936.

"Flood History: Southern Nevada's Worst Floods." *Las Vegas Review-Journal,* 20 August 2003.

"Flood Warning Given To Tenants." *Las Vegas Review-Journal,* 29 June 1993.

"Floods Damage Willow Beach." *Las Vegas Review-Journal,* 25 February 1993.

Fradkin, Phillip. "Edison's Nevada Power Plant Generates Ill Will." *Los Angeles Times,* 13 July 1972.

"Fresh Water Fishing." *Los Angeles Times,* 10 December 1965.

"From the National Capital." *Daily Evening Bulletin,* 19 December 1876.

Gallagher, Pat. "Eldorado Canyon Once Scene of Claim Jumpers, Two-Gun Killers." *Las Vegas Evening Review-Journal,* 18 March 1941.

Gardiner, Alexander. "Out of the Desert: An Empire." *American Legion Monthly* 17 (December 1934):18–21, 48–50.

"Geological and Wild Life Survey At Dam Started." *Las Vegas Evening Review-Journal,* 29 April 1936.

Goldblatt, Rochel Leah. "Boats Roll on Strip to Protest Lake Mead Closure." *Las Vegas Review-Journal,* 6 October 2013.

"Governors Due at Dam Rites." *Los Angeles Times,* 2 December 1952.

Grater, Russell K. "The Story of Davis Dam." *Arizona Highways,* March 1956.

Gustkey, Earl. "Resort Residents Fight Back." *Los Angeles Times,* 12 October 1979.

———. "Willow Beach Fight Not Over." *Los Angeles Times,* 20 June 1980.

Hayes, Trevor. "Boulder Residents Protest." *Las Vegas Review-Journal,* 23 May 2001.

Heinemann, E. H. "Colorado River History Told by Government Officer." *Las Vegas Evening Review-Journal,* 22 April 1936.

Holland, Steve. "Crime Rates in National Parks Soar." *Los Angeles Times,* 4 January 1981.

"Huge Davis Dam Project Nears Its Halfway Mark." *Los Angeles Times,* 7 June 1948.

Illia, Tony. "Bridge to Tomorrow." *Las Vegas Review-Journal,* 19 April 2009.

"Interior Department Approves Proposed $41,200,000 Dam." *Los Angeles Times,* 29 April 1941.

"Irrigation Making a New Sea." *New York Times,* 24 September 1905.

"Jet Ski Ban Goes Too Far." *Las Vegas Review-Journal,* 17 July 1998.

Johnson, Kirk and Dean E. Murphy, "Drought Settles In, Lake Shrinks and West's Worries Grow." *New York Times,* 2 May 2004.

Jones, Robert A. "National Parks: A Report on the Range War at Generation Gap." *New York Times,* 25 July 1971.

Kimak, John. "Boaters Say Proposed Fees May Be Unfair." *Las Vegas Review-Journal,* 7 October 1999.

———. "Boating Safety Report Shows Stunning Stats at Lake Mead." *Las Vegas Review-Journal,* 3 August 2000.

———. "Entrance Stations Will End Free Access to Lake Mead." *Las Vegas Review-Journal,* 5 August 1999.

———. "Fishing for Answers from Willow Beach Hatchery." *Las Vegas Review-Journal,* 1 August 1996.

———. "Flood Danger Causing Controversy at Willow Beach." *Las Vegas Review-Journal,* 5 August 1993.

———. "Lake Mead Officials Face Problem of Increase in Crime." *Las Vegas Review-Journal,* 4 March 1993.

———. "NDOW Outraged Over Ban on Stocking Trout in Mohave." *Las Vegas Review-Journal,* 28 April 1994.

———. "Rainbow Trout Production Resumes at Arizona Hatchery." *Las Vegas Review-Journal,* 19 January 2003.

———. "Rangers Have Busy Year at Lake Mead." *Las Vegas Review-Journal,* 5 February 1998.

———. "Repair Costs Increasing with Recurring Vandalism at LMNRA." *Las Vegas Review-Journal,* 15 October 1992.

———. "Services May Cease at Willow Beach." *Las Vegas Review-Journal,* 23 December 1993.

———. "Trout Dying While FWS Weighs Policy." *Las Vegas Review-Journal,* 16 June 1996.

———. "USFWS Actions Don't Match Words." *Las Vegas Review-Journal,* 28 July 1994.

———. "Wildlife Report Reveals Need for Better Boating Safety." *Las Vegas Review-Journal,* 28 May 1992.

———. "Willow Beach Change Proposed." *Las Vegas Review-Journal,* 4 November 1993.

———. "2000 Statistics Reveal Lake Mead Rangers Kept Busy." *Las Vegas Review-Journal,* 17 June 2001.

"Lake Mead Burros to Be Moved." *Las Vegas Review Journal,* 28 March 1995.

"Lake Mead, Largest Man-Made." *Scientific American* 158 (February 1938):108–09.

"Lake Mohave Ready to Impound Water." *Los Angeles Times*, 1 December 1949.

"Landscaping of B.C. Building Begun." *Las Vegas Evening Review-Journal*, 18 February 1938.

"Las Vegas Bay Marina's Relocation to Horsepower Cove Begins." *Las Vegas Review-Journal*, 2 October 2002.

"Legal Intelligence." *San Francisco Daily Evening Bulletin*, 13 December 1856.

"Letter from Sacramento." *San Francisco Evening Bulletin*, 26 February 1863.

"Like Ripping Apart St. Peters to Sell the Marble." Advertisement. *New York Times*, 20 May 1971.

Lindsay, Leon. "A Happy Ending to the Saga of Grand Canyon Burros." *Christian Science Monitor*, 10 July 1981.

Loftus, Mary Frances. "Making The Parks More Fit." *New York Times*, 7 June 1959.

Love, Fred. "House OK's bill to Combat Invasive Species." *Las Vegas Review-Journal*, 20 March 2007.

———. "Official Urges Rapid-Response Tactics to Curb Invasive Species." *Las Vegas Review-Journal*, 8 March 2007.

Lukianoff, Greg and Jonathan Haidt. "The Coddling of the American Mind." *Atlantic*, September 2015, http://www.theatlantic.com/magazine/archive/2015/09/the-coddling-of-the-american-mind/399356/ (accessed Feb 19, 2016).

"Man Made Dimple." *Literary Digest*, 3 August 1935, 17.

Manning, Mary. "Better Cell Service Sought for Lake." *Las Vegas Sun*, 19 March 2004.

Martin, Don. "Fee Increase Proposed for Lake Mead is Unfair." *Kingman Daily Miner*, 21 April 2010.

"Matters on the Colorado River." *Salt Lake City Daily Telegraph*, 7 December 1867.

"Mission 66." *New York Times*, 26 February 1956.

"Moller, Jan. "Hoover Dam Bypass to Be Delayed Further." *Las Vegas Review-Journal*, 9 November 1999.

"Mountain Lions in Arizona's Line of Fire." *Las Vegas Sun*, 7 April 2006.

"Mr. Wirth's Departure." *New York Times*, 24 January 1964.

Mueller, Gene. "Shenandoah National Among the Most Dangerous Parks in U.S." *Washington Times*, 3 September 2003.

Niehus, Charley. "Fishing in Lake Mead and Lake Mohave." *Arizona Highways* (March 1956):4–7.

Oates, John B. "Conservation: Long-Term Plans." *New York Times*, 7 April 1957.

———. "Conservation: The Ten Year Plan." *New York Times*, 4 March 1956.

O'Connell, Peter. "Feds Choose Route for New Dam Bridge." *Las Vegas Review-Journal*, 9 January 1999.

———. "Study: No Bridge Means Woes at Dam." *Las Vegas Review-Journal*, 1 October 1998.

"Officers and Youths Clash at Yosemite." *Los Angeles Times*, 5 July 1970.

O'Neill, Alan. "Protect Lake Mead and the Legacy of the National Parks." *Las Vegas Sun*, 29 December 2012.

"Organization of the Pacific Railroad Convention." *San Francisco Daily Evening Bulletin*, 21 September 1859.

"Owners End Negotiations to Sell Hacienda to NPS." *Las Vegas Sun,* 8 September 2004.

Packer, Adrienne. "Bridge to Open to Traffic Sans Fanfare." *Las Vegas Review-Journal,* 20 October 2010.

———. "Hoover Dam Bypass Bridge Opens." *Las Vegas Review-Journal,* 21 October 2010.

"Paintball Play Damages Petroglyphs, Rocks Near Laughlin." *Las Vegas Review-Journal,* 25 March 2010.

"Park Officials Close Pearce Ferry Launch Ramp." *Las Vegas Review-Journal,* 26 August 2001.

"Park Riot Alert Funds Approved." *Los Angeles Times,* 10 December 1970.

"Park Service Eyes Rules to Ban Watercraft." *Las Vegas Review-Journal,* 20 September 1997.

"Personal Watercraft Ban at Lake Mead Postponed." *Los Angeles Times,* 29 December 2002.

Pesek, Margo Bartlett. "Trip of the Week: Willow Beach Fish Hatchery Offers Educational Trip." *Las Vegas Review-Journal,* 17 April 2005.

"Plan to Kill Mountain Lions at Lake Mead Draws Protests." *Casper Star-Tribune,* 9 April 2006.

"Pledger, Marcia. "157,000 Visitors Expected." *Las Vegas Review-Journal,* 28 May 1993.

"President Signs Boulder Dam Bill." *New York Times,* 22 December 1928.

"Progress Noted In Park Program." *New York Times,* 4 December 1960.

"Proposal Would Hike Fees for Lake Mead." *Boulder City Review,* 11 February 2015.

"Quick Work by Harriman: Trains Rushed to Colorado River Break After President's Demand." *New York Times,* 22 December 1906.

"Railroad to Retreat." *New York Times,* 4 July 1906.

"Redeeming the Colorado." *New York Times,* 25 April 1901.

Ritter, Ken. "Third Straw Uncapped to Provide Lake Mead Water to Vegas." AP, 23 September 2015. http://news.yahoo.com/third-straw-uncapped-lake-mead-water-vegas-033417377.html (accessed February 19, 2016).

"River to Get Big Plants of 8-Inch Trout." *Los Angeles Times,* 15 April 1966.

"Road Over Boulder Dam Open Tomorrow." *Las Vegas Evening Review-Journal,* 11 December 1935.

Rogers, Keith. "Boaters Finding Mussels a Big Pain." *Las Vegas Review-Journal,* 3 March 2008.

———. "Lake Mead Fee Collection Figures Show High Number of $5 Passes Sold." *Las Vegas Review-Journal,* 4 June 2001.

———. "Lake Mead Fee Stations Not Ready for Weekend." *Las Vegas Review-Journal,* 1 July 2000.

———. "Lake Mead Fees Could Rise." *Las Vegas Review-Journal,* 6 April 2010.

———. "Lake Mead Fifth in Accidents, Report Says." *Las Vegas Review-Journal,* 6 September 2003.

———. "Lake Mead User Fees Rising January 15." *Las Vegas Review-Journal,* 30 December 2010.

——. "Lake's Invasive Mussel ID'd as Quagga." *Las Vegas Review-Journal*, 13 January 2007.

——. "Multistate Quagga Containment Plan Considered." *Las Vegas Review-Journal*, 24 January 2007.

——. "Mussel Infestation Limited." *Las Vegas Review-Journal*, 17 January 2007.

——. "Plan OKs Personal Watercraft." *Las Vegas Review-Journal*, 9 January 2003.

——. "Ranger Snares Invasive Mollusk." *Las Vegas Review-Journal*, 12 June 2004.

——. "Residents Granted Reprieve." *Las Vegas Review-Journal*, 31 December 1993.

——. "Threats to Hoover Dam Assessed." *Las Vegas Review-Journal*, 16 September 2001.

——. "Willow Beach Dispute Flares." *Las Vegas Review-Journal*, 9 July 1993.

——. "Willow Beach Tenants Given Notice to Leave." *Las Vegas Review-Journal*, 27 January 1994.

Rogers, Keith and Natalie Patto. "Fee-Collection Stations Near Completion at Lake Mead." *Las Vegas Review-Journal*, 22 May 2000.

Saldana, Lupi. "Anglers Hit Jackpot: Trout, Bass Bagged on Colorado River." *Los Angeles Times*, 26 March 1965.

——. "Safe Boating Week Proclaimed July 4–10." *New York Times*, 24 June 1971.

Schwartz, David McGrath. "Authorities Putting Emphasis on Lake Safety." *Las Vegas Review-Journal*, 27 May 2006.

Simon, Richard and Judy Pasternak. "U.S. Considers Easing Ban on Guns in National Parks." *Los Angeles Times*, 23 February 2008.

Slivka, Steven. "Boulder City Casino Resurrected as Hoover Dam Lodge." *Boulder City Review*, 16 January 2015.

Smith, John L. "Casino Project Near Lake Mead Raises Issue of Sprawl." *Las Vegas Review-Journal*, 31 October 1993.

Sofradzija, Omar. "Dam Bypass Looking Up." *Las Vegas Review-Journal*, 19 August 2006.

——. "Two-Year Delay at Dam." *Las Vegas Review-Journal*, 25 January 2007.

Squires, Michael. "Hoover Dam Bypass: Officials See Need for Speed." *Las Vegas Review-Journal*, 2 October 2001.

——. "Hoover Dam Bypass: Work on Project Begins." *Las Vegas Review-Journal*, 22 October 2002.

——. "Hoover Dam: Agency Selects Bypass Route." *Las Vegas Review-Journal*, 19 January 2001.

——. "In Regard to Dam Bypass, Boulder City Must Choose Battles Carefully." *Las Vegas Review-Journal*, 22 April 2001.

——. "Residents Blast Bypass." *Las Vegas Review-Journal*, 18 April 2001.

"Stopover in Sunland." *Nevada Highways* 21:1 (1961):18–25.

Tavares, Stephanie. "Quagga Mussels a Toxic Threat to Lake Mead." *Las Vegas Sun*, 9 November 2009.

"The Colorado Controlled." *New York Times*, 12 February 1907.

"The Colorado Expedition." *New York Times*, 21 July 1858.

"The Colorado Restrained." *New York Times*, 31 July 1907.

"The Complete Colorado River." *Los Angeles Times,* 29 November 1970.

"The Pacific Railroad: Indian Tribes on Mr. Whipple's Route." *San Francisco Sun* and *New York Times,* 27 April 1854.

"The Threatened Outrage." *Pioche Daily Record,* 17 April 1873.

"The Wozencraft Project in San Diego County." *San Francisco Bulletin,* 3 December 1859.

"They've Streamed in Via Kingman to Cross Dam." *Boulder Dam Challenge,* 6 March 1936.

Torgerson, Dial. "90 Arrested In Yosemite Youth Rampage." *Los Angeles Times,* 6 July 1970.

"Tourist Records Broken for Dam." *Las Vegas Evening Review-Journal,* 6 March 1934.

"Tourist Travel to Dam is Increasing." *Las Vegas Evening Review-Journal,* 3 March 1934.

"Tourist-check Stations at Dam Planned." *Las Vegas Evening Review-Journal,* 25 February 1937.

"Tourist-check Stations Start Thursday Morn." *Las Vegas Evening Review-Journal,* 31 March 1937.

"Trout, Bass Action Moves Into High Gear." *Los Angeles Times,* 23 April 1965.

"Trout, Bass Share Spotlight." *Los Angeles Times,* 19 March 1966.

Vartabedian, Ralph. "The Law Loses Out at U.S. National Parks." *Los Angeles Times,* 23 January 2003.

"Visitors Banned From Power Plant at Boulder Dam." *Las Vegas Evening Review-Journal,* 8 December 1941.

Vogel, Ed. "Nevada Officials Receive Federal Grant for Hoover Dam Bridge, Other Projects." *Las Vegas Review-Journal,* 31 October 1998.

Wade, Betsy. "Practical Traveler: Staying Safe In the Wild." *New York Times,* 11 April 1999.

Walz, Jay. "Park Service Lists Gains." *New York Times,* 10 November 1957.

———. "U.S. Parks' Gains." *New York Times,* 9 March 1958.

"Washington Telegraphic Items." *San Francisco Daily Evening Bulletin,* 4 April 1878.

"Washington." *Arizona Weekly Miner,* 23 February 1877.

"Water Worries: The Drying of the West." *Economist,* 27 January 2011.

"We're Now A Step Closer to a Police State." *Las Vegas Review-Journal,* 2 May 2001.

Welch, William M. "West's Water Worries Rise as Lake Mead Falls." *USA Today,* 26 July 2014.

Wetzel, Charles. "Why Blame the Kids." *New York Times,* 15 August 1971.

White, Ken. "On Duty at Lake Mead." *Las Vegas Review-Journal,* 21 March 1994.

Wines, Michael. "States in Parched Southwest Take Steps to Bolster Lake Mead." *New York Times,* 17 December 2014.

Young, Walker R. "Boulder Lake Is Now Largest Man-Made Reservoir in the World." *Las Vegas Evening Review-Journal,* 24 August 1935.

———. "Hoover Dam: Purpose, Plans, and Progress of Construction." *Scientific American* 147 (September 1932):135.

"Youths Battle Park Rangers." *New York Times,* 6 July 1970.

"198 CCC Boys in B.C. to Begin Park Projects." *Las Vegas Evening Review-Journal*, 11 November 1935.

"100,000 Baby Trout Put to Bed, To Be Planted in River in January." *Boulder City News*, 19 September 1945.

PRESS RELEASES

Lake Mead National Recreation Area. "Effective Date on Personal Watercraft Closures Extended." Lake Mead National Recreation Area News Release, 6 September 2002.

National Park Service. "Invasive Mussel Update from Lake Mead National Recreation Area." News Release No. 2–07, Lake Mead National Recreation Area, 16 January 2007.

———."Live Zebra Mussels Found at Lake Mead." National Park Service News Release, January 10, 2007.

———. Overton Beach Impacted by Lowering Lake Levels." Press Release 65–06, Lake Mead National Recreation Area, 26 December 2006.

SPEECH

Roosevelt, Franklin D. "Boulder Dam Dedication Speech," 30 September 1935. Transcript in *Vital Speeches of the Day* 2 (October 7, 1935):25.

WEBSITES

"American Watercraft Association to Protest Closure." Boats.com. http://features .boats.com/boat-content/2002/08/american-watercraft-association-to-protest -closure/ (accessed January 5, 2015).

"Are National Parks Becoming Crime Havens?" ABC News, June 25, 2003. http:// abcnews.go.com/2020/story?id=123679 (accessed February 19, 2016).

Bureau of Reclamation, "The Bureau of Reclamation: A Very Brief History." http:// www.usbr.gov/history/borhist.html (accessed February 23, 2016).

"Invasive Mussels Threaten Lake Mead." MSNBC.com. 18 July 2009, http://www .msnbc.msn.com/id/31980811 (accessed April 23, 2010).

"I-Team: Lake Mead's Water Level Declines as Lake Powell's Increases." KLAS News, Las Vegas, Nevada. 9 April 2010. http://www.8newsnow.com/story/10815107/i -team-lake-meads-water-levels-decline-as-lake-powells-increase (accessed April 24. 2010).

"Lake Mead to Ban Personal Watercraft." KLAS News Now, Las Vegas, Nevada. 22 July 2002. http://www.8newsnow.com/story/867421/lake-mead-to-ban-person al-watercraft (accessed January 5, 2015).

"Lake Mead Water Levels Worry Observers." KLAS News Now, Las Vegas, Nevada. 9 April 2010. http://klas.dua1.worldnow.com/story/12286324/lake-mead-water -levels-worry-observers (accessed February 17, 2016).

"Las Vegas, Nevada: Crime Rates by Year." http://www.city-data.com/city/Las -Vegas-Nevada.html (accessed February 23, 2015).

National Park Service. "Annual Park Ranking Report for Recreation Visitors in 2012,"
    https://irma.nps.gov/Stats/SSRSReports/National%20Reports/Annual%20
    Park%20Ranking%20Report%20%281979%20-%20Last%20Calendar%20
    Year%29 (accessed February 22, 2016).

———. "Lake Mead National Recreation Area: Black Canyon Restrictions, Motor-
    ized Vessel Use-Willow Beach to Hoover Dam," http://nps.gov/lake/planyour
    visit/blackcanyonrestrictions.htm (accessed April 22, 2010).

———. "Lake Mead NRA: Annual Park Recreation Visitation," https://irma.nps.gov
    /Stats/SSRSReports/Park%20Specific%20Reports/Annual%20Park%20Recrea
    tion%20Visitation%20%281904%20-%20Last%20Calendar%20Year%29?Park
    =LAKE (accessed February 12, 2015).

———. "Meadview Area History." http://www. nps.gov/lake/historyculture/mead
    viewhistory.htm (accessed April 30, 2010).

———. "NPS Stats: Lake Mead NRA." http://www.nature.nps.gov/stats/viewReport
    .cfm (accessed April 26, 2010).

———. "NPS Stats: Ranking Report for Recreation Visits in: 1979–2009." http://www
    .nature.nps.gov/stats/viewReport.cfm?selectedReport=SystemRankingReport
    .cfm (accessed April 26, 2010).

———. "Storage Capacity of Lake Mead," http://www.nps.gov/lake/learn/nature
    /storage-capacity-of-lake-mead.htm (accessed February 22, 2016).

Repanshek, Kurt. "Lake Mead Mountain Lions." http://www.nationalparkstraveler
    .com/2006/04/lake-mead-mountain-lions (accessed February 20, 2015).

———. "Violent Deaths in the National Parks," http://www.nationalparkstraveler
    .com/2008/03/violent-deaths-national-parks (accessed February 23, 2015).

Southern Nevada Water Authority. "Third Drinking Water Intake at Lake Mead,"
    http://www.snwa.com/about/regional_intake3.html (accessed February 25, 2015).

U.S. Fish and Wildlife Service. "Willow Beach National Fish Hatchery." http://fws
    .gov/southwest/fisheries/willowbeach.html (accessed April 23, 2010).

Wlfs4ever, Mojave Red, and iamthesmf, "National Recreation Area Proposes Fee
    Increases," on Nevada General Fishing forum, http://www.bigfishtackle.com
    /forum/Nevada_Fishing_Forum_C39/Nevada_Fishing_General_F42/LAKE
    _MEAD_NATIONAL_RECREATION_AREA_PROPOSES_FEE_INCREASES
    _P919124/ (accessed February 17, 2015).

Index